£9.99

Language and Literacy

Irene Yates

Activities based on the Desirable Outcomes for under-fives

Ideas for planning, assessment and record-keeping

Photocopiable stories, rhymes and songs

Author
Irene Yates

Series consultant
Pauline Kenyon

Editor
Clare Gallaher

Assistant editor
Sally Gray

Series designer
Joy White

Designer
Louise Belcher

Illustrations
Rachel O' Connor

Cover and photographs
Garry Clarke

Designed using Adobe Pagemaker
Processed by Scholastic Ltd, Leamington Spa

Published by Scholastic Ltd, Villiers House, Clarendon Avenue,
Leamington Spa, Warwickshire CV32 5PR

3 4 5 6 7 8 9 0 8 9 0 1 2 3 4 5 6 7

With thanks to Military Road Lower School in Northampton and Rainbows End Nursery in Leamington Spa for allowing us to photograph their work with the children in the nursery.

The publishers gratefully acknowledge permission to reproduce the following copyright material: **Gina Douthwaite** for the poems 'Finger face', 'Begins with "B"' and 'Mouse' © 1998, Gina Douthwaite, previously unpublished; **Her Majesty's Stationery Office** for the use of text from the Department of Education and Employment/SCAA document *Nursery Education Desirable Outcomes for Children's Learning* © 1996, Crown copyright; **David Higham Associates** as the representatives of the Estate of Clive Sansom for the use of his poem 'The engine driver'; **Karen King** for the use of her stories 'Silent Simon' and 'The alphabet hunt' © 1998, Karen King, previously unpublished; **Johanne Levy** for the use of her songs 'ABC Boogie' and 'Tell me a story, little book' © 1998, Johanne Levy, previously unpublished; **Tony Mitton** for the use of his poems 'Kitchen sink sounds' and 'Listen around' © 1998, Tony Mitton, previously unpublished; **Irene Yates** for the use of her story 'Pots and tripes', her poem 'Hissssss' and her rewrite of the traditional story 'The house that Jack built' © 1998, Irene Yates, previously unpublished. Every effort has been made to trace copyright holders and the publishers apologise for any inadvertent omissions.

British Library Cataloguing-in-Publication Data
A catalogue record for this book is available from the British Library.

ISBN 0–590–53756–3

Contents

Introduction

Perhaps the greatest gift we can give our children is the gift of communication. It is the ability to communicate that allows the child to connect with the world. This book explains how the skills of language and literacy develop and make that connection happen.

By the time they come to pre-school groups or nurseries, most children are fairly fluent in their home language. This language is part of their identity and part of their understanding of 'self'. Their whole ability in language is tied up not just with learning, but with confidence and self-esteem. All of a child's experiences are transformed when they can be appropriately translated into words.

Children whose first language is not English particularly need to know that their language is valued – it is a part of them and it is how they communicate with the world.

The Desirable Outcomes

Throughout this book the Desirable Outcomes referred to are those published by the School Curriculum and Assessment Authority in *Desirable Outcomes for Children's Learning* for use in England. The ideas in this book can be applied equally well to the guidance documents on pre-school education published for Wales, Scotland and Northern Ireland. The requirements for Language and Literacy in the Desirable Outcomes are split into three specific areas of activity: Speaking and Listening; Reading; and Writing. These areas all combine and interact to develop the child's whole ability in language and literacy.

The Desirable Outcomes show very clear expectations of children's ability:

Speaking and Listening

In small and large groups, children listen attentively and talk about their experiences. They use a growing vocabulary with increasing fluency to express their thoughts and convey meaning to the listener. They listen and respond to stories, songs, nursery rhymes and poems. They make up their own stories and take part in role play with confidence.

These expectations, or targets, basically cover all the kinds of activities and tasks that the children might be encouraged to take part in.

In listening, they can be assisted to sit quietly, give people turns to speak, listen attentively and respond to what they hear.

In talking, they can be encouraged to talk through all their play and creative activities with other members of the group and with all adults and helpers, and to take turns in contributing to the conversation or discussion.

In role play, children learn how it feels to be someone else, to have a different self-concept and other duties or responsibilities; by pretending to be someone else they assume a greater ability to communicate others' needs and feelings, to feel differently about themselves and to empathise with others. They learn to adapt speech to different situations, use a widening vocabulary and think about how they are communicating.

Reading

Children enjoy books and handle them carefully, understanding how they are organised. They know that words and pictures carry meaning and that, in English, print is read from left to right and from top to bottom. They begin to associate sounds with patterns in rhymes, with syllables, and with words and letters. They recognise their own names and some familiar words. They recognise letters of the alphabet by shape and sound.

It is never too soon for children to become acquainted with books and stories, though, of course, some children will come into the group with a great deal of 'print' experience, having had stories, books and rhymes read to them from babyhood; others will come into it having missed out on this vital experience.

It is important to make the whole incident of 'story' a happy one from the beginning, so that the children learn to equate the listening and the sharing of story-linked tasks with pleasure and comfort and joy from the outset. This way, hopefully, they will always enjoy and want to be involved with the reading process.

Understanding and assimilation of the concepts of print – orientation, matching letters, matching words, even page-turning – do not come to all children at the same time or at the same stages of development. Much depends upon their ability to discriminate both visually and aurally. They can be shown over and over again during 'storytime' until they absorb the idea without even knowing that they are doing so. Young children are active, not passive, learners – they need to be given opportunities to 'have a go' for themselves.

Writing

In their writing they use pictures, symbols, familiar words and letters, to communicate meaning, showing awareness of some of the different purposes of writing. They write their names with appropriate use of upper and lower case letters.

Again, not all children will develop these abilities at the same time. Much here will depend upon the extent of their gross and fine motor development, as well as hand and eye co-ordination. Play activities, such as threading beads, using pegboards, dressing dolls, constructing models with bricks, using paintbrushes and crayons and so on, will all help to develop these skills.

The ability to communicate meaning will depend upon how far the children can verbalise their own expressions of feeling, ideas and events. If the children are unable to put their ideas into words and to talk them through when they are speaking then they are going to find it very difficult to make those words appear on paper!

Integrated learning

Speaking and listening, reading and writing are the main means of children learning anything, so the more competent the early learner is in language skills then the better he or she will learn.

It is impossible for children who do not understand a set of instructions – in whatever subject area – to be able to follow them, so they need to be able to understand what they hear and what they read. As they move upwards into school, more and more of the instruction or knowledge children are expected to assimilate appears in the form of print.

In their daily lives, children need to be able to understand the world around them, and to associate with that world. They do this largely by talking and listening. If their abilities in talking and listening are restricted, then their world, rather than being enriched, will be limited.

Planning

The *Desirable Outcomes for Children's Learning* are a nationally agreed set of benchmarks for the under-fives, and 'inspection' is the evaluation of what the children achieve in relation to those benchmarks. This will involve taking into account the children's progress towards the learning outcomes, their attitudes towards learning and personal development, the quality of teaching and any other aspects of provision made for Language and Literacy which might affect quality or standards.

The more you plan, the better you will be able to assess exactly what each child is achieving, and the more easily you will be able to recognise individual needs as they arise.

Planning needs to take into account children with special needs, children with communication difficulties, children whose mother tongue is not English, and the planned curriculum needs to show how it enables these children to make progress. More of this is covered in Chapter 2.

Planning your resources

Contexts for talking and listening can be created within all the areas of the group environment. Some specific important resources are: equipment for practical activities (sand, water, construction materials and so on); home corner and other role-play areas; book corner (and books placed in other areas – a simple cookery book in the kitchen corner, for example); cassette recorders and cassettes; telephones; dressing-up clothes; puppets; games and play equipment; a carpeted sitting area where children can listen to stories and share experiences; labels and signs in the environment.

Whatever the children are doing, language is always the background and the key to it because the thinking process uses language. One of our tasks is to help children to develop their language skills in order to develop their thinking skills.

Safety

Young children need constant and careful supervision. Be vigilant and try to anticipate hazards – if sand or water is spilled, clean it up immediately; do not allow a child to build a model in an unsafe place, such as behind the door, and always keep the room tidy and clean.

Ensure that the materials the children work with are suitable for the age range and supervise the children closely when they are working with small or sharp objects. When taking the children on an outing check your local authority regulations for the correct adult to child ratio. Make sure you are aware of any allergies, illnesses or other health considerations concerning the children.

Equal opportunities

Ensure that your own language presents a positive role model to the children – avoid phrases such as 'two strong boys' or 'three little girls to clear up' and so on.

Your choice of books is crucial for reflecting your equal opportunities policy. Ensure that your resources show people of all cultures and backgrounds, in non-stereotypical roles. Provide books that show, for example, men doing domestic chores, women at work, and both boys and girls as the main protagonists in adventure stories.

Demonstrate a positive attitude to all races and cultures during discussions and encourage people from different ethnic backgrounds to visit your group to talk with the children.

Working with parents

It is important to establish good links with parents and to give them the feeling that their views are welcomed and that their help is appreciated.

To remind parents how crucial language skills are to the child's development as a whole, and to draw attention to the importance of their own role in helping to develop them, the following strategies can be used:

* Display notices showing 'Way in' in different languages, if appropriate.
* Hold informal meetings for discussion of language and literacy development. Explain to the parents how you intend to teach the children early skills and how they can help.
* If possible, get together a little 'Reading' booklet telling parents how they can make reading at home fun.
* Label displays, showing what individual children have done (but don't let this become a competition).
* Display photographs of the team, with their names and changes of rota, and encourage the parents and children to refer to it. Pin up notices asking for any input you may need or perhaps describing the 'theme of the week' and so on.

How to use this book

This book sets out to show you how to plan a language curriculum to give the greatest benefit possible to the children in your group. The initial chapters will show you how to plan, taking account of children's stages of development, and how to assess and record the learning taking place. There are activity chapters devoted to speaking, listening, reading and writing, as well as photocopiable activity pages which may be used as extensions to some of the activities.

The book also has a section on rhymes, stories and songs, with explanations of how they assume their importance in the development of language and literacy skills, and ideas as to how they can be used, given in the activities.

The other six books in the *Learning in the Early Years* series deal with the other areas of the Desirable Outcomes:

* Mathematics;
* Personal and Social Development;
* Knowledge and Understanding of the World;
* Physical Development;
* Creative Development;
* Ready for Inspection.

chapter one

Planning

This chapter will show you how to analyse the children's needs and plan for them. It will help you to use your resources to maximum effect by showing you how to make long, medium and short-term plans, incorporating explorative, collaborative and imaginative play.

Why plan?

It is easy, within an unstructured pattern, to assume that all of the children's needs are being met by the provision of play, creative activity and story when in fact the language elements of those activities are not being recognised and used to stretch the children to their optimum potential.

When planning for children whose first language is not English, be aware that, as users of at least one language, they are already competent listeners and communicators. In some ways they may be advantaged because they will probably have greater linguistic awareness than children with only one language.

Good planning allows you to evaluate the outcome of your provision, recognise the children's levels of development and plan consistent experiences to meet their needs while they play, talk and investigate at their own pace.

Where to start

Remember that all the children may be starting from a different point; some will have very good communication skills and others may have very few. You can build upon the abilities of each child and extend their competence by taking account of:

* the needs of listeners – do they understand? Do they have enough knowledge? Is there a need to be more explanatory?
* the aptitude of each child for turn-taking;
* the willingness of the children to join in purposeful discussion;
* the ability of different children to organise (in their heads) what is being said;
* opportunities to build a more extensive vocabulary for each child.

In order for a curriculum plan to remain consistent and be acceptable to everyone, when planning is in progress all members of the team should meet to discuss and pool ideas. Each member's input should be valued and welcomed; where inconsistencies or variances exist they should be fully discussed and some agreement reached.

All members of the team should understand the principle of 'concepts, skills and attitudes'. Many psychologists believe that none can be learned without the others and that children learn all three at the same time. Concepts can be defined as 'knowledge' or 'knowing what' and 'knowing that'; skills may be defined as 'knowing how' and include all the activities that children learn through practice; attitudes are their feelings about what they are learning. Attitudes are absorbed as children are learning concepts and skills, and will always govern how they feel about, and are motivated to work at, a particular area.

Thus, in the language curriculum you might be teaching new vocabulary (concepts), through writing (skills), and developing good attitudes towards language and writing by making it a fun activity. Or you might be teaching skills, for example hand-eye co-ordination, while they are learning concepts of colour through a satisfying creative task (such as making a necklace).

Planning might begin with the team asking themselves questions, such as:

* How long are we planning for?
* Who else is involved in the planning?
* Are we looking at all aspects of language development as a whole or are we looking at Speaking and Listening, Reading and Writing as separate factors?
* If we look at each separate resource (water play, home play, outside play and so on) can we brainstorm ideas for Speaking and Listening, Reading and Writing for each area?
* Can we identify the key concepts, skills and attitudes we wish the children to develop in each of these areas?
* Do we need more resources?
* How can we involve parents and provide links with home?
* Are there specific activities or goals we need to set? Should these be for all children, or for individuals?
* Do we need any extra professional development in this area, for example are there courses we could attend?

Speaking and Listening	Reading	Writing
Maths – language for position and ordinal number. smaller than/larger than fat/thin long/short more than/less than	Read 'The house that Jack built', develop idea of patterns in things and words.	Water play – make a 'big book' with the group on 'Water'. Write sand patterns, patterns in collage...

Once the brainstorming and discussion have evolved, show this stage of the plan simply. Divide a large sheet into three with the headings Speaking and Listening, Reading and Writing. Under the headings list the opportunities that are to be found in other areas of the curriculum or in your setting.

An alternative approach would be to divide the sheet into areas of the curriculum and resources, each listing the opportunities for development in Language and Literacy (see chart below).

Neither of these have to be the final plan; they are just the starting point. Remember though that however the plan emerges it is important that evaluation becomes a part of it.

Language in:				
Mathematics	Personal and Social Development	Knowledge and Understanding of the World	Physical Development	Creative Development
Words – fat/thin, long/short, in/out, smaller than/larger than, less than/more than, big/bigger/biggest	Language for friends and family. Buy books with multicultural element for book corner.	Discussion of home and family – the immediate environment, descriptions of routes to group...	Words – on/off, over/under, through, behind/in front of, up/down, inside	Make puppets for Three Bears story; make puppets for retelling other stories.

Stages of planning

Your plans can be written in the way that suits your team best. You may like to have flow diagrams or charts, or you may like to have sheets of paper, showing each stage in the planning process, fastened into a booklet, or it might be appropriate to keep your plans written on cards in a box file. Try and come to a consensus of opinion within the team, so that the plans are accessible to everyone.

It is important that you keep all your plans as 'evidence', ready for inspection. Since inspection will be only a 'snap-shot' in time, the inspectors will check long, medium and short-term plans to look for coverage and progression, and to get a good idea of how different children's needs are being met.

Long-term

Long-term planning means looking at the language needs of the children over a period of, say, the whole year and deciding exactly what goals you would like to aim at for each child during that year. It should also recognise key events, for example a farm visit, which provide the framework for language activities.

Formulate some easily explained aims; the following are just a few examples – it's quite possible that once you start you'll have a job to stop! Try at all times to think in terms of concepts, skills and attitudes. For example, find opportunities for each child to:

Speaking

* speak in small and large groups with confidence;
* speak and exchange ideas with peers and with known adults with confidence.

Listening

* sit quietly in a group and listen attentively;
* listen to and follow verbal instructions;
* listen and respond to nursery rhymes, stories and poems.

Reading

* follow the direction of print;
* understand how a book works;
* respond to print with confidence;
* learn the sounds of letters.

Writing

* use pictures to show a meaning;
* develop a positive attitude towards writing;
* form the letters of their name.

Write out your long-term aims clearly, and decide how you are going to split them over the year. Are you going to work on all aims at all times during the year, or are you going to split the year into sets of sessions and work on some of the aims for part of the time?

It can also be useful during this long-term planning session to think about the resources that you have available, and see where they fit into the plan. Make a list of what you have that can be used towards each goal, and a list of what would be useful if you could possibly acquire it. Sometimes this kind of planning leads to ideas that might never have been considered before, such as inviting speakers into the group or making visits.

Medium-term

Armed with your long-term plan, you can now decide how the content of your provision, or curriculum, will be organised. Of course, you will need to take into account other areas of the curriculum. But for working out a language curriculum everything can be cross-curricular, so this should not be difficult. For example, could you take a topic or theme approach that might incorporate all areas of the Desirable Outcomes?

Themes chosen should, ideally, offer opportunities for new learning in all areas of the curriculum, as well as reflect and acknowledge the children's own interests. They should aim to extend the children's present knowledge and offer opportunities for the children to involve themselves in investigation and problem solving.

Discuss and choose a series of topics or themes and decide how best to exploit their language possibilities. After deciding whether each should last one or two weeks, your medium-term plan might begin like this:

Weeks 1 and 2: theme – ***Colours***
Week 3: theme – ***Water***
Weeks 4 and 5: theme – ***Homes***

Now break down each theme into ideas:

Theme – ***Colours***		
Speaking and Listening	*Reading*	*Writing*
Colour poems. Colour stories. Identifying colours. Learning names of colours. Looking for colours. Favourite colours. Rainbow song. Colouring pictures. Descriptive words.	Labelling colours. Initial sounds of colour words. Words that rhyme. Colouring names. Choose a colour list in the painting corner.	Patterns in different colours.

From this medium-term planning, you are now ready to look at the day-to-day activities, the organisation, and the methods you will use to include the span of ability within the group and how best to make sure that each child is involved.

Short-term

This planning will help you to work out what will happen in each session, how the children will move through the organised activities, who will assist them with each task and how you will evaluate what has happened during the session.

From the above mid-term plan, the team would need to assign one member to look through resources for the stories, rhymes, poems and songs that relate to the theme, and to collect them together and acquaint everyone with them. You would then need to work out exactly how you would organise your resources, your different play areas, and how you would fit in the normal group routine that the children are used to. This stage of the planning would, in fact, incorporate the everyday tasks and activities of the group, while taking into account the different needs and abilities of all the children. It may be necessary to present tasks in different ways to different children, depending upon the level of support they need.

Try to support bilingual learners with audio cassettes and books in home languages. You may have outside assistance to help you with this, or you may be able to involve parents or other members of the community.

At all stages of these activities the children should be offered opportunities to play, talk, interact, experience and investigate in their own time. Members of the team would be observing the children during the activities in order to record their learning, and evaluate their progress. At all times, all adults working with the children should be clear about the aims of the activities and the way in which these activities should be approached.

Assessment and evaluation

A lot of your assessment will take place as you work with and observe the children every day, but it needs planning into the curriculum so that it is undertaken systematically. Records linked to planning will provide a good record of what has been covered and will help you to plan for progress, making sure that you are not spending too long over some curriculum areas at the expense of others.

Chapter 3 gives more information on keeping records.

Planning for inspection

Part of the inspection process, for Language and Literacy, is direct observation of the children's activities, during which the inspectors assess how well the children watch and listen to each other and other adults, how well they use materials and other resources, and how well they can represent and record their learning. Therefore your short-term plans need to show all the expected activities.

The inspectors want to see progress and gains in knowledge, understanding and skill, and they have to evaluate whether these gains are sufficient, good or poor in relation to prior attainments. Keep your plans in order, so that the inspectors can see how you have detailed and organised plans for progress.

In any pre-school situation Language and Literacy must receive a high priority, with the emphasis on children learning through talk. The inspectors expect to see, as a normal event, staff engaging children in both planned and spontaneous conversation. This will include members of the team and other adults participating in the children's role play, and supporting and extending their imagination and use of language. They also expect staff to read and share books with individuals, as well as small and large groups, in both a spontaneous and a planned way as the children undertake various activities. Team members should also talk with children as they work, about their drawings and the symbols they use for words and letters. All of these activities can be shown on your short-term weekly or daily plans.

Your long-term plans will show that this is how you expect to operate. Where there are children learning English as an additional language, the inspectors will take into account the different problems they may encounter, and the fact that they may need to develop extra confidence before they speak in English, but they will expect that the teaching and activities in your plans will be geared to support the children in a positive way. They would also hope to see the team understanding that many of the children will have considerable language ability in their home language and that these abilities are being taken into account.

Teamwork and support

Everyone in the early years group needs to feel that their contribution is valued and compatible with the group's general aims and philosophy. When those aims are written down clearly, then the whole team will have a thorough knowledge of how the group is expected to work and what is expected of the individual.

This is particularly true in the area of language development, where it is possible to leave so much to chance that no positive and structured support to progress ever takes place. It isn't enough to say to members of the team, or parents or volunteers, 'talk to the children' because they may need guidance in how to do so and how to extend the children's learning.

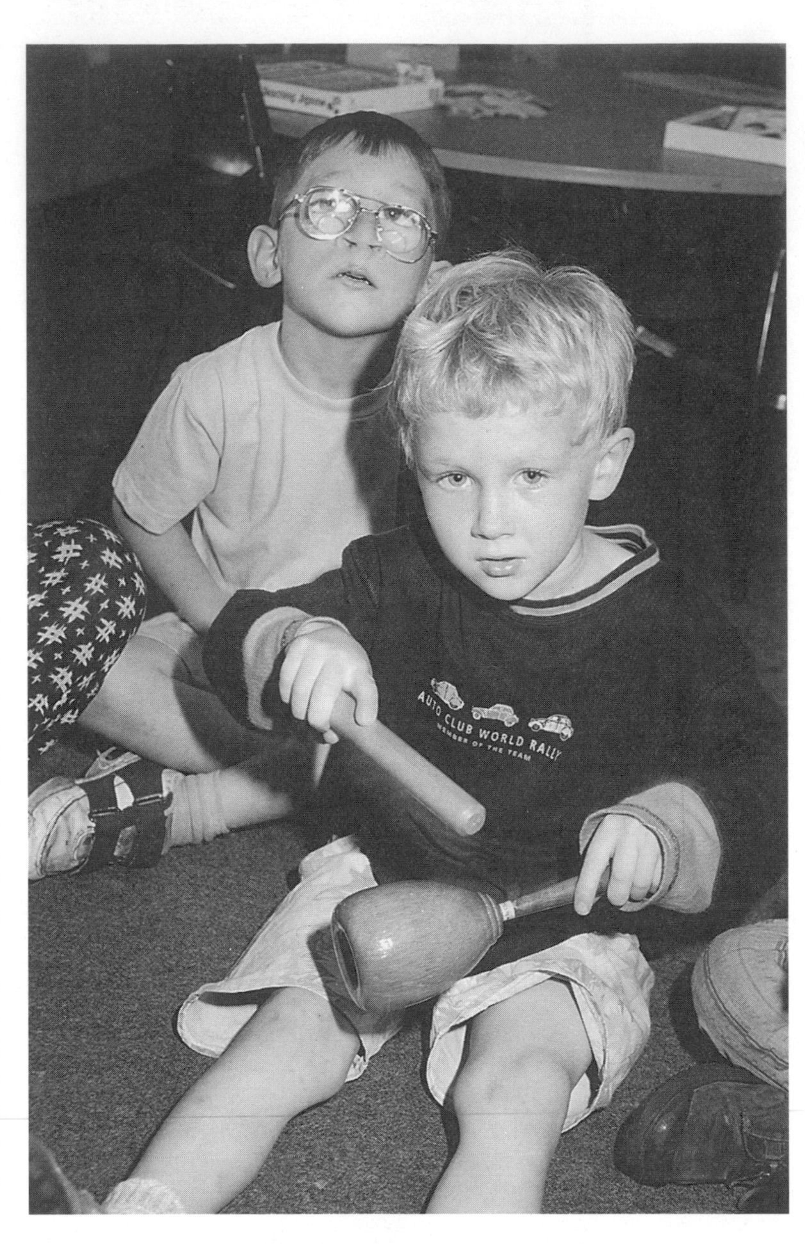

Your long-term plans can be explained to them so that they have a good idea of what the language curriculum is all about, then they can be shown how those plans translate into daily activities. It's a good idea to have short but regular discussion sessions with all helpers and volunteers because talking about the issues involved in planning for language development will, in itself, make them feel involved and reinforce the fact that they are partly responsible for the children's progress.

Remember always that you are planning for a well organised and effective learning environment. Your objective is to engage the children in activities within your group that are both challenging and appropriate to their needs and interests.

Summarising the planning process

1 Establish period of learning.
2 Formulate goals or aims.
3 Consider the needs and interests of the children.
4 Select topics or themes.
5 Brainstorm ideas for each topic.
6 Identify all the language possibilities.
7 Translate into activities and tasks.
8 Decide on organisation.
9 Decide how the theme will begin and end.
10 Decide on how and when the children's learning will be evaluated.

chapter two

Child development

This chapter will show you how children first acquire and then extend their ability and understanding of language. It explains how early support and guidance is crucial to the acquisition of lifelong skills for interpretation, organisation and control of language.

Language development involves a number of skills, which develop and mature together and form a whole. These skills are basically:
Receptive language – sometimes called comprehension or understanding. Understanding always comes before verbalisation, at every stage of language development. Even from babyhood, children understand much more than they can actually put into words.
Expressive language – this is the child's ability to use words, phrases and sentences.
Phonology – the ability to use the sounds of speech in the right places, to make the words sound different from each other.
Prosody – being able to change volume, speed and intonation when talking.
Fluency – being able to talk in a smooth way, without hesitation or much repetition.
Use of language – being able to select words and construct sentences that make meaning, and eventually being able to read and write.

How children learn language

A child's first language is its cry as a baby. Babies cry to communicate their needs – whether they are hungry, thirsty or tired, for example. Most parents learn to distinguish very early on between a baby's different cries.

Eventually a baby learns to babble. It begins to make the sounds of some of the consonants – 'd' for instance, or 'g' or 'm'. When babies have two or three consonant sounds, they will put them together so that they make two-syllable combinations – 'dadda', 'gaggah'. At this stage, the baby often understands the idea of turn-taking, and will make a sound, wait for the parent to respond, then make another sound. The parent begins to 'interpret' what the baby is saying and models the words he or she thinks the baby is trying to say. The baby mimics the parent, and gradually the babbling sounds increase into strings of sounds, which will be needed for later talking.

At first, babies use the words with which they are most familiar – 'mummy', 'daddy', 'drink', 'car'. By repeating the word, the parent helps to shape the words. This constant repetition helps the baby to learn to put two words together. At this stage, the baby's 'talk', accompanied by lots of babbling, is sometimes called 'scribble talk' or 'jargon'. Positive reinforcement and lots of praise help the baby to persevere with its efforts to communicate.

By about two years of age, the child can produce a group of words in their correct order, that others can understand, for example 'Daddy gone shop'. The typical adult response is 'That's right, daddy has gone to the shop, hasn't he?' In this way the adult acknowledges the meaning of the child's words, reinforces them and expands upon the language.

From about the age of three, most children begin to absorb grammatical knowledge from the language that is used to them, and learn to construct longer, more complex sentences, using the correct tenses for verbs as well as intonation to help express their meaning. This is true of any language and children with more than one language are absorbing the rules of each simultaneously.

Speaking and listening

Most children develop their abilities to speak and to listen without any direct instruction or teaching. Language is their method for finding out about themselves and about the world. Their language evolves because they listen, question, make suppositions about what they understand and interpret the responses that are made to them. In turn, their language ability gives them a tool for making sense of new experience.

Reading and writing

As the children progress, more and more teaching and learning will depend upon their reading and writing skills. Right from the beginning, literacy skills can be taught alongside listening and speaking skills. The sub-skills the children need for reading and writing are:

* visual and auditory discrimination – the ability to distinguish between different shapes and different sounds;
* visual and auditory memory – the ability to remember, recall and identify different shapes and different sounds;

* orientation – the ability to follow a direction with their eyes;
* hand and eye co-ordination – the ability to match hand movement with eye movement;
* fine motor control – the ability to hold and control tools such as paintbrushes, pencils and so on.

Remember that it is never too soon for books and stories. The sharing of these, with a familiar person, in a contented and happy way, will do much to provide the child with a firm foundation for literacy. The child will need help to talk through pictures, picking out details, to 'read' the text, to work out how the pages turn, perhaps even which way up the book should be, but all this help is just part of a very long sequence of events that make up the continuum that is 'learning to read'. It is not something that begins at five and ends at the age of eleven but something that begins very early in a child's life and never really ends.

In the same way as for reading, children can learn to share writing with adults even from babyhood. With constant repetition they will soon learn to understand what 'writing a letter to Grandma' means; they will appreciate that the marks on the paper mean words that you can speak and that the marks remain the same. They will soon want to make the marks for themselves. Playing at writing is an important stage in the development of their skills. Their feelings about writing and about themselves as writers will be influenced by the messages they receive at this early stage. Thus, if they are encouraged to have a go and their products are valued, they will build positive attitudes towards writing.

The power of play

Young children learn a great deal about the world through play activities. Every play enterprise leads to the building of thinking skills, and thus language and literacy skills.

Children's ability to play develops gradually, but once they have developed the facility to take part in play, by taking turns (such as in 'peep-o') and in mimicking (such as in 'pat-a-cake'), they have the capability to change focus, rather than being totally absorbed in one object or working specifically to their own agenda. They can change their focus, from an object to a person playing with them, back to the object. They are now open to absorb more of the language that will enable them to understand and to talk. The more use you can make of 'play', the more language they will absorb.

Through play, children learn to share and join in, and initiate and follow 'rules'. They add to their motor skills and problem-solving skills, and learn to communicate more and more.

Imaginative play activities, such as drawing and little games, provide the children with opportunities to explore and experiment with literacy. Often the children will begin to make up stories which they re-enact, either with others or alone. This kind of play is a firm foundation for the literacy skills they will develop, particularly if they are allowed to feel confident and powerful in taking risks. If, at this point, they can be provided with writing and reading materials, those materials will become part of the 'game' and this will help to support the good attitudes towards reading and writing that are essential for encouraging early skills.

English as a second language

Children who have learned one language, their 'home' or 'first' language, have already absorbed much of the knowledge they need to help them become competent language users. They already understand how meaning is imparted in the sounds and structure of language; they know that language is made up of separate words and the order in which those words are used (syntax). Therefore they are quite open to learning a second language which is a common language for play or other activities within the group. They have already developed their thinking skills and their ability to process their perceptions in 'language' (rather than in 'English') and they need all the support you can offer them to build on these solid language foundations. Try to find ways of strengthening their 'language' learning by providing audio cassettes, books and adult or peer interaction in their home languages.

It does not make it easy for young children to learn a second language if their first language is ignored. In fact, it makes it much more difficult. They can't just leave their first or home language behind them and learn to speak all over again. Rather, they need the first language to be their foundation and support to give them the confidence to go forward in their endeavours to communicate in a second language. Bilingual adults or other children are of great help in explaining new concepts or ideas to early second language learners.

Where several children speak the same language they should be encouraged to use their preferred language for talking through ideas. It does not confuse the children, on the contrary they are able to move in and out of their home language with an obvious understanding of the needs of their audience.

from *Teaching and Learning in Key Stage One* by K Norman (National Curriculum Council).

The group's attitude towards the children's first or home language is of great importance to their development as second language users. Home languages are a powerful and major part of the child's identity and history. If they are dismissed or ignored then the child will also feel dismissed and ignored. Positive attitudes towards bilingualism will do much to build up the children's confidence as language learners.

Remember that bilingual children are continually hearing English spoken on television and in their daily environment, such as in shops and supermarkets – possibly the family speak more than one language at home anyway. Good home-school links with the group are particularly important. Parents may be willing to translate stories and rhymes, to provide songs on tape and to produce bilingual resources for the group. If you can make a positive approach to using their expertise then you are showing the children that all languages are valued and that all languages are an asset and of benefit to their users.

There need not be a huge worry about children learning second languages if planning and resourcing is done with care. If the language environment is natural, consistent and stimulating, children will pick up whatever languages are around.

from *Child Language, Learning and Linguistics* by D Crystal (Arnold).

It is important that all the children feel free to be themselves and to interact with their peers. No child should ever be allowed to feel isolated or marginalised because he or she is not as confident in English as those in his or her peer group for whom it is a first (and probably *only*) language. Conversely, it is just as important that those children who are monolingual learn to value languages other than their own, and efforts should be made to positively encourage good attitudes.

chapter three

Assessment and record-keeping

It is important to be able to assess the individual child's progress and to spot any language problems early. This chapter explains assessment and shows you how to keep simple but effective records.

The importance of assessment

Advancement in language is monitored possibly more closely than any other area of intellectual development in the early years because, of course, everything else really depends upon it. A child who cannot communicate an idea, feeling or an explanation cannot demonstrate her knowledge. It is crucial, therefore, that you have some understanding of the way in which competence in speaking, listening, reading and writing develop.

You have to be aware of the long-term aims of language development and ensure that short-term goals achieved by the children indicate progress towards those long-term aims. This knowledge will help you to plan all your specific language activities to build upon the knowledge and abilities that the children already have. It will also help you to recognise and provide subject-specific vocabulary, enabling you to build language development into all areas of the curriculum.

You need to be able to gather the same information about children's knowledge and skills for a whole range of skills, and record them in such a consistent way that you can obtain a set of results which can be compared with the results of other groups. This will then give information about 'relative pupil progress' or how one group might achieve alongside another group. For example, the backgrounds of the children of two different groups may put one group at a disadvantage even though they work through the same activities. 'Relative pupil progress' is known as 'value-added information' and is an important part of baseline assessment.

National Baseline Assessment

Statutory baseline profiling means that every child will be assessed in the same way. Though this may be seen by some group leaders as a hurdle to be tackled it is also a way of screening the children and pinpointing early difficulties that may predict future learning problems.

In language development the children will be assessed in three areas: Speaking and Listening, Reading and Writing. There will be an equal entitlement for all children to be assessed, including those children in the group for whom English is not a first language. Any special educational needs of the children will also be taken into account.

The aim of baseline assessment is to provide an early understanding of each child's knowledge, understanding, attitudes and skills so that curriculum planning can be appropriate and provide learning opportunities to match individual needs. Information gathered from such assessment is also invaluable for planning the purchase and organisation of resources.

Linking planning and assessment

Although you will be informally observing and monitoring the children's ability in language all the time, it is important that you fit formal times for assessment into your curriculum plans. You also need to know, at every point of assessment, exactly what it is that you are assessing.

Your programme will need to give planned opportunities for all the children, over a period of time, to display their abilities.

Speaking and Listening

Try to identify what the children can do rather than what they cannot do. Once you start assessing with clear objectives you will find that many children are much better communicators than has been acknowledged.

Although you should be able to monitor the children's listening and speaking competence across the whole curriculum, be careful to consider other factors. For instance, the nature of the audience or the listener can have a considerable effect upon children's discussion. The type of task and the children's interest in it can affect their performance, as can the child's gender, ethnicity, the peer group, the personality of the child, and so on. Try to make the circumstances of your formal assessments as conducive as possible to the children.

It is helpful if you build up a record of achievements over a length of time, noting some of the children's spoken interactions within a normal session. Indicate on your short-term or weekly planning the kind of tasks and activities that will give the children opportunities for using talk in lots of different situations with a range of different partners and audiences.

Look through your plans for chances to observe the children as they:

* listen and respond to direct questions;
* pay attention to simple messages, rhymes, stories, songs and so on;
* talk about what they are doing, including commenting upon their own play;
* talk about things that interest them with peers and familiar adults;
* listen attentively and talk about their experiences in small or large groups.

All of these opportunities for assessment can happen while the children are carrying out normal session activities. Go back through your short, medium and long-term planning and look for opportunities where they exist, then mark them on your plans and work out how you can fit the children to them. You may need to undertake some focused assessment tasks with small groups or with individuals.

Reading

Reading is not just about the ability to decode the words on the page, it is about enjoying the activity and wanting to do it, so the child's pleasure in literature is an important part of his or her progression in literacy skills.

Discussing and sharing a book with a child will give you a lot of information about the child's reading behaviour. It is quite easy to keep a notebook record of books the children like and what their reading strategies are. (For instance: 'points to the words; follows left to right; retells the story confidently'.) You can also keep individual home-books to go home with the child. This book could have a list of books shared at the group and at home with a space for comments from other adults and, perhaps, a comment from the children themselves.

Look through your plans for chances to observe the children:

* listening to story sessions;
* participating in story sessions;
* browsing and choosing books in the book corner;
* looking at books alone or with other adults and children;
* demonstrating awareness and use of print;
* bringing 'story' into play situations.

These situations will show you how, when and what the child reads and, again, opportunities for these observations can be marked onto your short-term plans.

Keep track of this early development by noting down such strategies as demonstrates an interest in books, chooses to look at books, is able to recog familiar words, is able to retell a story using picture clues'.

Writing

Although some of the children may be too young for formal writing lessons, your aim should be to develop their enjoyment and competence in writing and to enable them to explore personal reasons for writing.

Obviously your long and short-term planning should take into account the need for a good writing area with plenty of resources (see Chapter 8) and the provision of opportunities for children to 'write' for all kinds of different reasons. You need to be giving them the chance for a variety of written activities during other play activities, and praising, displaying and sharing the writing with others.

You will need some kind of framework for assessing the children's writing abilities well before they can actually be described as 'competent writers'. The first factor of this framework needs to be 'attitude'. What is the child's attitude towards writing? Does he or she:

* have a positive feeling about writing?
* embark upon 'writing' as a free activity?
* become involved with 'writing' and sustain that involvement?

A child's enthusiasm for writing will largely depend upon your own attitude. If you show the children that writing is a normal and enjoyable activity, something that can extend an experience, they will quickly take their cue from you.

Your observation of the children will need to be over quite a long period. Ask questions such as:

* Does the child express ideas in speaking and then 'pretend' to write them down?
* Does the child use his or her imagination to create stories and so on?
* Are the child's marks and symbols organised as though he or she is writing?

There may be many spontaneous moments when the children suddenly turn to writing as a means of recording something they have done or seen or want to remember. Keep a notebook handy to jot down these occurrences and to make comments about how the children worked on them – did they work together, alone, with confidence? Did they 'read' what they had written back to you? Was the writing straight across the page, going in the right direction, showing signs of letter formation, word formation, sentence formation?

If the children are bilingual they may be able to 'write' in English and in their home language. Give them the opportunity, praise their work and share it with the rest of the children.

The assessment process

When to assess

Try to assess all of the children at least once during each term, so that you have a good record of their starting point, their progress and their final achievements. If this proves impossible or unmanageable, work out how you could assess twice during the year. Do your first assessment when they have settled into the group and found their feet.

The three photocopiable assessment and record-keeping sheets for Language and Literacy on pages 73–75 will help you to maintain assessment without it being too much of a burden.

Who assesses?

Everyone who is involved with the child needs to be able to contribute their own observations and to know what they should look for. They will therefore need to be given a very clear picture of what exactly is being observed. Photocopiable pages 73–75 can be used as a guide to the skills in Speaking and Listening, Reading and Writing that they should be assessing.

How can we assess?

After finalising what is going to be assessed and when it will take place, the next step is to decide who will be assessed. You can then designate someone to do the assessing (it may be yourself), giving them a clear list of targets (for example, 'holds the book the right way up, 'reads' the story from the pictures, moves in left to right direction') with a tick list for recording.

You could also assess the children on a rolling programme, selecting two children each day and asking the team to observe and note what they are able to do. In this case, you would make a file for each child, each page headed with a specific target from the Language and Literacy area of the *Desirable Outcomes for Children's Learning*. Members of the team can then make notes appropriately. The final stage should be a session where you discuss the files and the notes together. This rolling programme is a good strategy because it will help you to identify gaps in individual children's development and the team can then plan activities for them as a specific programme.

How can we record?

Keep your paperwork as simple as possible so that it doesn't overwhelm you. If you are keeping files for each child to cover the whole curriculum, your language and literacy pages can be easily slotted into them. Collect some samples of writing from the children and keep them in the file, making sure you have written the date on them and any comments you need to make (for example, 'Rashed wrote this letter spontaneously in the post office corner').

Involving parents and carers

Parents and carers need to understand or to be reminded that they play a crucial role as the first educators of their children, so you need to keep them involved and informed about your assessments. They need to know how their child is developing and achieving, and it is important to always stress the positive factors.

Give them plenty of practical ideas that you know will help their children's progress. For example, for the child's reading development, suggest books they might take home and share with the child as a partner for reading and, if necessary, show them how to elicit the child's response to story. All of the links that you make with home will have a beneficial effect on children's learning but you must show parents how to make the 'work' enjoyable.

chapter four

Talking and listening

Children cannot learn to communicate on their own – their interaction with other people will affect their opportunities to learn and their ability to talk effectively. The activities in this chapter are designed to help them learn to understand thoughts, to recognise feelings and to connect with other people through talk.

Share it with me

Learning outcome

To have the confidence to offer more and more spoken information.

Group size

Four or five children.

What you need

A selection of toys.

What to do

Organise the children so that they are sitting in a circle with you. Place the toys in your lap and explain to the children that they are going to play a game where they will pass the toys around the circle and each person has to say something. In turn they will have to try to remember everything that has gone before, and then add something new.

Do the first two or three rounds as examples so that the children understand how to play the game. For instance, if the first toy is a car:

ADULT: This is a car. (*Passes the toy to the child on his or her left.*)

CHILD: This is a red car. (*Passes on the toy.*)

NEXT CHILD: This is a red car and it has four wheels. (*Passes on the toy.*)

NEXT CHILD: This is a red car with four wheels and I can play with it. (*Passes on the toy.*)

NEXT CHILD: This is a red car. It has four wheels. We play with it and I've got one at home the same. (*Passes on the toy.*)

And so on.

Questions to ask

Who can think of anything different to say that no one has said yet? Who can remember what (child's name) said? Who knows something else about red cars? What are real cars for?

For younger children

The children may find it difficult to remember all the information that has been repeated, so give them lots of prompting and help. The aim of the game is not to trick them but to help them to remember and recall.

For older children

Give out a toy to each child, and for each round start at a different point so that everybody gets a chance of beginning and ending the round. If a particular object is the cause of plenty of conversation see if the children can manage a second round.

Links with home

Describe the game to the parents and ask them to play it with the children on occasions at home.

Follow-up activities

* Encourage the children to talk about which was their favourite round.
* Play the same game, with the children choosing the items to pass round. Give them choices – 'Shall we begin with the car or the boat?'

What shall we do?

Learning outcome

To use a growing vocabulary and convey meaning.

Group size
Individuals.

What you need
Normal group resources.

What to do

Involve the children in a normal everyday activity, such as tidying things away. Take every opportunity to extend the children's language by showing interest, responding and waiting for them to return conversation to you, showing them, by using facial expressions, that you are expecting them to talk back. Always try to engage them in eye contact, so that you have their full attention.

Allow the child to lead the conversation, and adapt what you are doing so that you can share particular moments. Explain and describe, as you are doing things. Examples of this kind of sharing are:

BETH: Books.
ADULT: Oh, shall we put the books away, Beth? Where do you want to put them?
BETH: Shelf.
ADULT: Yes, we'll put them on the shelf, shall we? (*Look, and wait, for a response.*)

HASSAN: Outside.
ADULT: Oh, do you want to go and play outside, Hassan? What would you like to play on?
HASSAN: Swing.
ADULT: You want to go on the swing. Would you like me to push you on the swing? Shall I make you go up high? (*Look, and wait, for a response.*)

Questions to ask
What shall we do now? What shall we do next? Where shall we put these? What are we going to do with this? Where do these belong?

For younger children
Try to stay at a level, face to face, with each child in turn so that they sense your interest in what they are doing or saying. This approach will make it much more likely that they will include you in their activities, and they will be much more aware of what you are doing and saying.

For older children
Interpret each child's attempts to communicate so that they feel they have been heard and know that you are trying to understand them. When you feed back the correct action or word to a child, he or she will begin to remember it. Give the children space by waiting for their responses, so that they feel their participation in the conversation is expected and valued, and they recognise when they should take their turn.

Follow-up activities
* Involve the children in as many activities as you can, including making the drinks and fetching the biscuits. Give them turns, and encourage them to describe what they are doing.
* Make cards with pictures showing different actions in the sequence of normal routines and ask the children to explain what is taking place.
* Play games with the cards – place them out of sequence and then let the children put them in the right order.

Links with home

Emphasise to the parents the importance of talking through everyday events, such as doing the shopping, laying the table and so on, rather than letting them happen with no explanation.

Good questions

Learning outcome

To listen attentively and respond to others.

Group size
Three or four children.

What you need
Home corner and resources for role play.

Preparation
Prepare the home corner for the children to enact a home play situation.

What to do
In the home corner let the children take on different roles, doing various home-corner tasks such as laying the table, preparing a meal, packing away the shopping and so on. As the children are playing (for example, at packing away the shopping) ask questions that show an interest in what they are doing and elicit a response: where did you shop? Who puts the shopping away at home? Why does the cheese go in the fridge? Where should we put the biscuits? These questions will develop children's thinking skills.

Encourage them to make choices or decisions by asking them if they need any other items. Ask them questions that begin with who, what, where and why.

Try to avoid questions that will halt the conversation, such as 'What's that?' or 'Who's that?' or questions that answer themselves such as 'This is a cup, isn't it?'

Questions to ask
What are you doing? What's that for? Who did you see? Where would you like to go? What did you do in the water play? What did you do in the sand play?

For younger children
Show them that you are waiting for a response by looking at them with anticipation, waiting for them to take a turn. It is especially important with younger children to make sure they realise that they have your interest.

For older children
Try to think of questions that will make good conversational hooks and encourage the children to share experiences with you and the other children. Finding the right question isn't always easy but the children's responses will show you how well you have succeeded.

Links with home

Encourage parents and carers to ask open-ended questions at home to elicit good language responses and to develop speaking ability.

Follow-up activities
* Encourage the children to talk with the group about what they have been doing in the home corner/water play/sand play and so on.
* Can the children think of questions to ask each other which will help them to describe their experiences?
* Make a display frieze showing children playing in the home corner and write questions to label the frieze. Read the questions with the children and help them to answer them.

What's happening?

Learning outcome

To understand more about what is experienced, and to say new words.

Group size
Individuals.

What you need
A sheet of paper, felt-tipped pen.

What to do

This activity will enable you to help the child to find more language to describe his or her activities. First choose an activity that the child really enjoys. In the centre of your sheet of paper draw a picture of the activity, for example building with blocks. Around the picture make seven spaces, headed 'Label', 'Describe', 'Explain', 'Pretend', 'Talk about feelings', 'Talk about future' and 'Project'.

Talk about the activity with the child. Listen to the language the child uses to describe what he or she is doing, and on your paper jot down the words he or she uses, under the appropriate headings. This will help you to 'hear the gaps'.

After the activity take time to fill in the spaces and think about what specific language you could add to help the child learn more about the activity. You can write down words or phrases or ideas that you think will extend the child's language. Next time you do the activity have a look at your sheet and try to follow your ideas for extending learning.

Questions to ask
What else could we build? How could we build it? What did (child's name) build? What did you build yesterday? Which building is your favourite? Why? When did you build it?

For younger children
It might help to jot down some of the vocabulary that they already have, before you work out which words you could add for them. Don't try for too many words at a time, as this will be confusing to them.

For older children
Give the children plenty of opportunities to pick up new words from you as they are working, for example you might say, 'Let's collect all the bricks together. Let's put them on top of one another. Let's give each yellow one a red one on top.' When you have used a phrase two or three times, say the beginning of the phrase and leave time for the children to finish it.

Follow-up activities
* Armed with your picture and the words you want to feed in, share the activity again, making opportunities for using the specific words or language and inviting the children to respond and use them back to you.
* Find other opportunities to feed in the specific words or language. For instance, change a building activity from bricks to a construction kit and show how new words work in different contexts.
* When the children learn new words make a point of telling some of the others, for example 'Beth has learned a new word today' Give the child the opportunity to use the word, and give lots of praise.
* Read the story of 'Silent Simon' on photocopiable page 83 and talk about it.

Links with home

Send a written note to parents that says '(Child's name) has learned these new words today...', and ask them to support you by helping the child to recognise opportunities for using them.

Sock on, sock off

Learning outcome

To understand positional words.

Group size
Six to eight children.

What you need
A sock, two boxes (one bigger than the other), table, small pieces of card, felt-tipped pen.

What to do
Put the boxes side by side on the table; one of the boxes should be open. Tell the children that they are going to play a sock game and demonstrate the game to them. Put the sock on the table and say 'sock on'. Take the sock off the table and say 'sock off'. Put the sock in the large box and say 'sock in'. This way the children should grasp the idea of how the game is played. Check that they all understand the following words: in, out, on, off, up, down, under, over.

Start the game by placing the sock in a particular position and saying where it is. For example, put the sock in the smaller box and say 'sock in'. Choose a child to take the next step in the game. When he or she takes the sock from the box, all the children should say 'sock out'. The child then puts the sock in another position and says the relevant words. If he or she is wrong, another child in the group should be allowed to take a guess. If the words are still wrong, let the first child try again.

Take turns throughout the group, getting the game to go faster and faster. Encourage the children to think of other positional words and use them, such as 'beneath', 'beside' and so on.

Questions to ask
Whose turn is it next? What happens if we move the boxes? Can we find a different object for doing 'in', 'out', 'over', 'under' and so on? What about 'here' and 'there' – can we find something for those words?

For younger children
Children often need lots of repetition before they have absorbed a word and want to attempt to use it. Find as many ways as possible of using the same word

by changing the sock for a different object. This will enable the children to begin to understand that the positional word means the same no matter what word comes before it.

For older children
Write the words out carefully on card and put them in the relevant places, telling the children what they say. This will help them to begin to recognise the words.

Follow-up activities

* Turn the game round by giving the sock to one child and asking the others to suggest the word; the child then follows their instruction.
* Draw pictures of the places and the sock. Cut out the sock and let the children glue it into appropriate positions on the pictures and label them.
* Play 'Guess where the sock is' – everybody closes their eyes while someone else hides the sock, then they try to find it. The first one to give the correct positional word has the next turn.

Links with home

To increase awareness of the use of positional words, send a note home: 'Today (child's name) has been playing a game using 'in', 'out', 'on' and 'off'. Please listen to her using these words.'

What do I hear?

Learning outcome

To listen carefully and to identify familiar sounds.

Group size
Whole group.

What you need
A quiet space, cassette recorder, cassette.

Preparation
Tape a selection of familiar sounds, for example a doorbell, a door knocker, the phone ringing, a tap being turned on, loo flushing, radio, clock, microwave, children chattering, children singing, feet walking, cat miaowing and purring, dog barking, car starting up, traffic passing, paper tearing, a purse closing, a jar opening.

What to do
With the children sitting in a group, talk about some of the familiar sounds that they hear every day. Ask them to think about the different kinds of noises they hear at home: what noises do they hear inside the house? Can they think of noises made by machines inside the house? What noises do people make inside the house? What about noises outside the house, in the garden or the yard? Do they hear machine noises outside? Can they think of animal noises? What kinds of noises do they hear in the street? Do they ever hear people's voices outside? They will probably enjoy imitating a lot of the noises.

Play your cassette of recorded sounds. Ask the children to listen carefully to each sound and put their hand up if they can recognise what the sound is.

Questions to ask
When do we hear this sound? Where do we hear it? Do we know what it means? Who heard this sound today? When? Where? What happened when you heard it? Who thinks they'll hear this sound today? Where do you think you'll hear it? Why?

For younger children
Focus on only a few sounds at a time. Give the children plenty of time to listen to and consider what each sound might be. If they need to discuss it with another child allow them to do so.

For older children
Use some of the more unusual sounds. If they're not sure let them listen two or three times. Try to dissuade them from telling each other what the sounds are, encouraging everyone to try to work it out for themselves.

Follow-up activities
* Teach the children the poem 'Kitchen sink sounds' by Tony Mitton on photocopiable page 77.
* Ask the children for suggestions of sounds that they might record in the group. Ask an adult to listen to the sounds and 'guess' what they are.
* Tape-record the children playing with various resources and then play the cassette back to them.
* Listen to a story that you have pre-recorded and in which you have inserted sound effects in appropriate places.

Links with home

Invite family members to the group to listen to some of the sounds and see if they can guess what they are. This will help them to understand the importance of developing listening skills.

What do I mean?

Learning outcome

To role-play activities, to guess other peoples' actions and explain what they are.

Group size
No more than ten children.

What you need
A large space in which the children can move about freely.

What to do
Ask the children to think of another person whom they could pretend to be. It could be someone they know, somebody in the community, somebody on the television, or somebody from a book, a story or a nursery rhyme.

Decide upon who you are going to 'be' to demonstrate the actions of another person, such as a person who has an easily recognisable job. Sit the children in a circle and ask them to watch you as you act out the part of someone else. Tell the children who you are being. For instance, you might be a postwoman. Your actions should concentrate on one activity, such as emptying the postbox into your postbag.

Explain that the children should put this one action you have carried out into words. Go round the circle, starting with the child on your left, and continue until everyone has had a go.

Questions to ask
Who do you think you could be? Think of all the things that person does. What would be a good action to act out? Can you guess who someone else is as soon as they begin? How good were their actions? Can you find a way to improve the actions?

For younger children
It is probably best to limit the actions to well-known and familiar things, such as family and household chores to start with, before widening the children's scope to the group and the community.

For older children
Encourage the children to use their imagination to choose a wider range of people to be, with a greater variety of tasks to perform.

Follow-up activities
* Help the children to overcome shyness by role-playing lots of different people and doing activities all together, as movement activities.
* Ask the children to draw pictures of who their role-play characters are and what they do.
* Mime the actions of the people to the tune of 'Here we go round the mulberry bush', encouraging everyone to join in the game.

Links with home

Tell the children to perform their actions to those at home and ask them to guess who they are and what they are doing.

What do I see?

Learning outcome

To describe objects.

Group size
Whole group.

What you need
Lots of different objects.

What to do

Talk to the children about how you can describe things. Explain to them that describing is telling someone what something is like. Give an example or two by describing individual children, what they're dressed in and so on. Show the children one or two objects and ask them to help you describe them.

Now play a game. Ask one child to be 'on' and the rest of the children to close their eyes. The child who is 'on' should describe things he or she can see, but should not give the name of the object. No one is allowed to speak to help. The child cannot say what the object is for or what it does.

Hold up an object. Help the child who is 'on' by running your finger along its shape. If it has wheels or circles, run your finger around them. If it has, for instance, four wheels, point to one, two, three, four to help them count. When the child has exhausted all possibilities of what he or she can see, ask if anyone can tell what the object is. If someone guesses right they have the next turn. If no one guesses, then you will have to give another clue.

Questions to ask

Can you see this inside your head? Try and picture it. What shape is it? How big or small is it? What colour is it? What do you think it is made of?

For younger children

Start with very simple objects, and make sure that all the younger children have plenty of opportunities to speak, to listen and to guess.

For older children

Let them choose objects by themselves – encourage them to choose ones that they think will be difficult for the others to guess.

Follow-up activities

* Play the game the other way round. Ask a child to choose an object and let the other children ask as many questions as they wish until someone guesses.
* Put some objects into a feely bag. One at a time, let the children feel each object and describe it. See if they can guess what the objects are.
* Ask the children to give you descriptions of the clothes their friends are wearing.

Links with home

Send a message home such as '(Child's name) has been learning how to describe things. Encourage her to describe her favourite toys to you.'

Do it myself

Learning outcome

To talk through the sequence of an activity.

Group size
Four or five children.

What you need
Items for making a salad – lettuce, carrots, cress, tomatoes, cucumber, salad-dressing (leave this out if the children don't like it), colander, vegetable knife (adults only), plate, bowl, kitchen roll, paper plates, access to water.

What to do
Explain to the children that you are going to make a salad to share. Check that the children know the names of the salad items and the names of the pieces of equipment. Say the words, asking the children to repeat them. Make sure the children all have clean hands. Explain how you will make the salad, giving the children a clear sequence. Talk the children through the activity, and share the making of the salad with them. First, take the lettuce apart, and let them help to wash the leaves, tear them and pat them dry with kitchen roll. Cut and slice the tomatoes and cucumber. Cut the carrots into sticks. Wash the cress. Let the children put all the ingredients into a bowl, pour in some dressing and toss the salad with their hands.

As they help you to prepare the salad, ask them at each stage of the activity, 'What is the next bit we're going to do?' At the end help them to remember the sequence.

Questions to ask
What should we do first? Now what do we do? What are we using to hold the lettuce while we wash it? How can we dry the lettuce? How much dressing should we pour in? How can we toss the salad? Why must we do it very carefully?

For younger children
Talk about what the vegetables feel like, whether they are soft and squashy or hard and crunchy, whether they are easy to handle or difficult. Talk about which vegetables the children like and dislike.

For older children
Ask the children to tell you what they did, trying to remember and organise the sequence of the activity, individually.

Links with home

Encourage family members to let the children help with preparing food at home, and tell them how helpful it is for the children's language development.

Follow-up activities
* Eat the salad together.
* Think of other sequencing activities you could do together, such as making sandwiches or washing toys' clothes.
* Prepare a set of directions for doing other activities, using pictures instead of words. See if any of the children can follow the activity.

Can you do what I do?

Learning outcome

To watch carefully, imitate and describe actions.

Group size
Seven or eight children.

What you need
A doll, a hat, a ball, keys, a spoon, a lunch box, a big cardboard box, paper.

What to do
Organise the children so that they are sitting in a circle with you. Put all the objects within your reach. Make sure the children know what they are.

Explain to them that you want them to watch you carefully and copy what you do. Do several actions, such as pointing your finger, shaking your head, licking your lips, opening your mouth, yawning, making a fist and touching the floor. Ask the children to imitate each movement.

Tell them to think about the things that you are doing. Do several of the actions again, but this time let the children take it in turns to verbalise the actions.

Take the objects one at a time and make an action with each one. You might pat the doll, put the hat on the doll, bounce the ball, rattle the keys, stir with the spoon, open the lunch box, climb in the big cardboard box, screw up the paper.

Again, let the children imitate (by miming) your actions, and then verbalise them.

Questions to ask
Can you do this? What did I do with the doll/hat/spoon? Can you think of something different to do with the objects?

For younger children
Give them plenty of time to mimic your movements one at a time. Leave a pause between each movement. Let them all have a chance to put the movements into words. Give them turns to verbalise a new instruction, with the other children making the action.

For older children
When they're used to the game, verbalise the movements yourself without doing them, and ask the children to do them quickly, one after the other, so that you might be saying, 'Make a fist, wave bye-bye, lick your lips, jump up and down, open your mouth' and so on quite quickly, with the children listening intently in order to carry out the instructions.

Links with home

Encourage parents to talk with their children about what they're doing, for example: 'Now we've packed all the shopping in the car, we're going home.'

Follow-up activities

* Change the objects and think of different actions.
* Take photographs of the children miming some of the actions, ask them to describe them, then label the photos.
* Teach the children how to play 'Simon says'.

chapter five

Developing expressive language

The activities in this chapter are designed to enable children to feel confident when they express themselves, to help them to learn through discussion, to help them to listen to, evaluate and respect the opinions of others, and to become competent in listening and speaking.

Who are we?

Learning outcome

To develop the ability to describe being part of the group.

Group size
Whole group.

What you need
Space for discussion.

What to do

Sit in a circle together to have a discussion. If necessary, do some work first on 'Who am I?' so that the children have a good understanding of what it means to be their unique selves. (See the next activity for appropriate work on this theme.)

Tell them you are going to talk about what is 'mine' or 'theirs' and what is 'ours'. Ask them to give you examples of things that are unique to them, for example can they show you things that they could label? (My shoes, my coat, my peg, my picture, my toy, my friend...)

Explain that things that belong to all of them can be called 'ours'. What can they see that is 'ours'? (Our room, our toys, our books, our crayons, our paints...) All these things belong to us and are 'ours' because 'we' have this room for 'our' times together.

Extend the discussion by asking the children if they can think of things 'we' can all do to keep 'our' room tidy. How can each child be really part of 'we'? What can they do to help the group as a whole? Tell them that 'We all belong to this group; we all share this room; we all help each other'.

Questions to ask

When the children are not part of the group, when they are at home, they are part of a different group. Who makes up each child's home group? Can you think of something that could be a 'my' thing and an 'our' thing? Can you tell me something 'I' can do that 'we' all could do?

For younger children

Put plenty of emphasis on the caring and sharing aspects of 'mine' and 'ours'.

For older children

Can the children see that the 'we' in the group and the room are part of a bigger 'we' outside the group and the room?

Follow-up activities

* Ask the children to paint pictures of themselves and their friends.
* Can they paint or draw pictures of the things they like to share?
* Play games such as 'Here we go round the mulberry bush', 'Lucy Locket' or 'The farmer's in his den' in which everyone can join.
* Give the children photocopiable page 88, 'What can we do?', and let them respond to it, speaking to an adult helper.

Links with home

Invite parents and other family members into the group to talk about the kinds of things they do, where they live and so on.

Who am I?

Learning outcome

To use growing vocabulary to express thoughts and convey meaning.

Group size

Three or four children.

What you need

Magazines and catalogues (with plenty of pictures of food, places, clothes, toys, animals and games), scissors, PVA adhesive, large sheets of paper.

Preparation

Prepare a large sheet of paper for each child. At the top, write 'Who am I?' At the bottom, write the child's name.

What to do

Explain to the children that part of what makes each of them themselves are their preferences, the things that they like. Tell them that they are going to build up a montage of ideas, individually, to show who they are by the things that they like.

Give the children plenty of opportunities to talk about the things they like. Help them to sort, cut out, arrange and stick pictures onto their paper to show: food I like for breakfast, food I like for lunch, food I like for tea, places I like to go, favourite kinds of clothes, favourite toys, favourite animals and favourite games.

Finally, give each child time to show and talk about their personal poster to the rest of the group.

Questions to ask

What games do you like best to play? Who do you play them with? When do you play them? What do you do when you play them? What do the other children do? Encourage the children to add information all the time to what they are telling you.

For younger children

Provide the children with pre-cut illustrations – if they cannot find items that they would like, help them to draw pictures instead. Then help them to sort their cut-outs and pictures into separate categories on their personal poster.

For older children

Encourage older children to sort their own illustrations and locate them under the separate headings with much less help. They might like to put their selections into pages of a home-made book, rather than just making a poster.

Follow-up activities

* Pair the children to talk about and share their posters.
* Do a group count of favourite things – for example, how many children have blue as their favourite colour?
* Display the children's work for them to enjoy and to help them build up a good self-image.
* Take opportunities to reinforce to the children that they are individuals in many ways, not just in their physical appearance.

Links with home

Play a 'Favourites game'. Ask parents or carers to choose something that they think is the child's 'favourite' before looking at the posters or books to see if their choice has been included.

How does it feel?

Learning outcome

To listen and respond to nursery rhymes.

Group size
Five or six children.

What you need
Space for the children to move freely, paper, crayons.

Preparation
Make sure the children have a fairly good repertoire of nursery rhymes and simple poems.

What to do
Choose a nursery rhyme or poem that the children know. Tell them that they are going to act it out.

Say the rhyme first, to make sure all the children know exactly what the focus of the activity is going to be, then do the rhyme again with the children role-playing.

Repeat the nursery rhyme several times so that each child can be different people in the nursery rhyme, for instance in Humpty Dumpty they can act it the first time being Humpty Dumpty, then the second time being all the king's horses and all the king's men. If they want to continue with pretend plays and stories, let them do it, because it will help to create empathy and let them identify with the characters.

Afterwards, sit the children together and ask them to draw a picture of when they were Humpty Dumpty and another picture of when they were all the king's horses and all the king's men. There should be some subtle differences in the pictures. Encourage them to talk through their pictures with you as they are drawing them.

When they have finished the pictures, give them turns to tell each other what it felt like to be each of the different roles, who they liked being most and why.

Finish with everyone singing or saying the nursery rhyme together again.

Questions to ask
Which people are in the nursery rhyme? Who did you like being best? Why? What did it feel like when you changed over to be someone else? Who feels happy/sorry/pleased for Humpty (for example)? Why? Who feels happy/sorry/pleased for all the king's horses and all the king's men (for example)? Why?

For younger children
Join in the role play with them, taking a part yourself and leading the children slowly through the rhyme if necessary.

For older children
Encourage the children to talk through what happens in the rhyme in sequential order before they begin the role play.

Follow-up activities
* Encourage the children to tell you the 'story' of their pictures, and write their words down for them so that they have 'retold' the rhyme in their own words. Read them back to the children after you have written them.
* Play 'Who am I?' Each child thinks of a character from a nursery rhyme and gives a brief idea of what happens in the rhyme. The children guess who it is.
* Play 'I'm thinking of a rhyme...' and give the children just one clue which won't give the game away too easily. They have to ask you questions: 'Are you an animal?', 'Do you go to school?' and so on until they guess the rhyme.
* Read the poem 'Listen around' by Tony Mitton on photocopiable page 77.

Links with home

Send the children's pictures and words home, asking an adult to go over the 'story' with them so that they can talk about what happened.

How do I feel?

Learning outcome

To develop the ability to talk about feelings and emotions.

Group size
Three or four children.

What you need
Large mirrors, cassette recorder, cassette.

Preparation
Make a short cassette recording that has some happy sequences and some sad sequences on it. For example, for a happy sequence you might have a door being knocked, the door being opened and somebody saying 'Oh hello, how lovely to see you!'; for a sad sequence you might have the sound of something being dropped and broken, and someone saying 'Oh no!'

What to do
Set up the mirrors so that all the children can see themselves and you in them. Mime lots of actions and facial expressions for the children. You can do simple things such as combing hair, cleaning teeth, eating, smiling, laughing, pretending to cry, frowning, yawning, scowling. Invite the children to try and copy you, watching each other and their own facial expressions in the mirrors.

Ask the children to explain, individually, how someone might feel if they were showing a specific expression on their face. Play the cassette and stop at each sequence to ask the children what kind of expression the person speaking might have on his or her face at that time, and how he or she might feel.

Questions to ask
How do I feel when I pull this face? Who can show me the face of someone who is really happy? How about really sad? How about cross? Or puzzled? Or not understanding something? How about someone who has hurt themselves? Someone who is lonely? Someone who wants to be friendly?

For younger children
Explain to the children that although their feelings are unique to them others may have similar feelings. Explain that they should try to express their feelings. Give them as many different words for feelings as they can manage.

For older children
Draw out their ability to express themselves by asking them gently, 'Tell me a time when you had this kind of face – what happened to make you feel like this?'

Links with home

Suggest that the children discuss the kind of things that make them happy with people at home.

Follow-up activities
* Teach the children the poem 'Finger face' by Gina Douthwaite on photocopiable page 78.
* Act out short sequences in which the children make someone really happy or in which someone is sad, worried or injured.
* Make finger puppets, giving them happy or sad faces.
* Sort through magazines to find pictures of faces that have different expressions, cut them out and assemble a montage.

Talking machine

Learning outcome

To develop the ability to express thoughts, feelings and emotions.

Group size
Pairs.

What you need
A large cardboard box (big enough for a child to sit in), junk modelling materials, Sellotape, cotton reels, scissors, card, paper, an egg-timer or a clock timer.

What to do
Explain to the children that they are going to make a magic talking machine and that they will be able to use it themselves. Anyone who is inside the talking machine just talks and talks. Show the bits and pieces of junk modelling material that you have and ask them if they know what the talking machine will look like. This will help them to plan and to problem solve.

Make the talking machine together. Cut a hole on one side of the cardboard box, telling the children that this will be the speaker hole. Make the box look 'realistic' by including complicated detail with lots of cotton-reel knobs and dials. Then add a pretend 'on' and 'off' switch.

When the machine is made, the children should take turns to be the speaker or the questioner. The speaker sits inside the box. The questioner sits on the outside of the speaker hole and switches the machine on. Then he or she asks the speaker questions. The questions can be simple ones such as 'What's your name?' or 'How old are you?' or they can be more involved, such as 'Tell me about your favourite toy'. Once the machine is switched on and the speaker has heard the question, the speaker should speak out. After about five minutes (two timings with the egg-timer or five minutes on the clock), the children should swap over.

Make a rule that the machine cannot be 'switched off' until the time runs out. Encourage the children to vary their discussions – you may need to give them themes to talk about after they have had one or two goes.

Questions to ask
What do you think a magic talking machine should look like? Can you think of any other talking machines that you know? How can we decide who is going to be first inside the machine? What kind of things might the questioner ask the speaker?

For younger children
You may have to make the machine yourself, letting the children help you to do the finishing touches. Help the questioner with questions that will elicit good answers.

For older children
A large part of the language development will come from giving them as much free rein as possible in designing and making the talking machine.

Follow-up activities
* What would happen if the box became a talking *story* machine?
* What would happen if you put two talking machines speaker to speaker and they were both switched on?
* Encourage the children to speak simple things, such as their names and ages, onto a cassette and play it back for them to hear their own voices.
* Make junk model cassette recorders.

Links with home

Let the children take turns to take the magic talking machine home, to involve parents in the activity. Ask the children to give you some feedback.

Stand next to me

Learning outcome

To increase vocabulary of positional words.

Group size
Whole group.

What you need
A tambourine or other percussion instrument, plenty of space.

What to do
Familiarise the children with positional words such as 'in front of', 'behind', 'next to', 'at the side of'.

Explain to the children that they are going to move around the room – hopping, skipping, twirling, running, walking and so on – to the sound of an instrument and that you want them to stand still when you stop playing.

Have a sequence of movements in mind, such as walking first, then hopping, then skipping, and tell the children what that sequence is. To start with, all the children should freeze into 'statues' and then move as soon as they hear the instrument, moving around the room in an appropriate manner to your chosen sequence. When you stop playing the instrument the children should stop and freeze again.

Explain that next time the group starts to move you would like some of the children to go to a particular place when you stop playing the instrument. One child will be the person who is 'on' and will choose three children and tell them where they should go when the beat stops – for example, 'Ayesha must go and stand in front of the radiator' and so on. (For less confident children, you may need to collaborate with them about who will stand where and tell the group the chosen locations yourself.) Let the first child to do this choose the next child to be 'on'.

Play the instrument in different ways, for instance soft or hard, slow or fast, to encourage the children to vary their movements. When you have exhausted the sequence of movements the game is over.

Questions to ask
In what different ways could we move? Can you hear whether you should move fast or slow? Who can freeze into such a good statue that they don't move at all? Can you make your movements a little bit different from everybody else's?

For younger children
When you decide upon the sequence of movements, bear in mind how well they can remember the instructions. Help them by giving them two movements to begin with, then trying three, then four and so on.

For older children
Work on further words, particularly 'left' and 'right'.

Follow-up activities
* Extend the children's vocabulary by helping them to give more complex instructions – 'turn around', 'jump up and down', 'crawl through' and so on.
* Give the children some toys to place in different positions when they have listened to verbal instructions.
* Play 'What is it?': say 'I can see something that begins with the sound of... and it's next to/underneath/on top of... the table (for example) – what is it?'

Links with home

Ask people at home to help their children with using positional words when they are putting their toys away and so on.

Let's write a song

Learning outcome

To make up a song and present it with confidence.

Group size
Five or six children.

What you need
Props such as toys and items of clothing (if required).

Preparation
Make sure that the children are familiar with two or three simple songs and know the tunes.

What to do
Sing a familiar song with the children, perhaps 'London Bridge is Falling Down'. Choose a song that has less than ten different key words and lots of repetition. Suggest to the children that they could help you to make up new words to the song.

Choose words that relate to people, objects and actions the children know, and encourage them to think of appropriate words themselves. Use props where you can. For instance, for 'London Bridge' choose one of the children to build a bridge with blocks, and sing, 'Jamie's bridge is falling down, falling down, falling down, Jamie's bridge is falling down – Gemma will fix it!' For 'Jingle Bells' you could use clothing and sing 'Hats on heads, hats on heads, hats on children's heads, Oh what fun it is to wear our hats upon our heads!'

Don't worry about getting the words to rhyme, just work on words that fit into the rhythm pattern – the children will love them!

Questions to ask
Who can think of a good start for our new song? Can we make another verse? What else can we sing about? Who can we sing our new songs to?

For younger children
Use more props, as they will help the children to think of good ideas. Try to work out actions and gestures that the children can do to go with the words of the songs.

For older children
Allow the children the opportunity to add their own lines and also to anticipate what might be coming next. Ask the children to think of actions and gestures themselves to accompany the songs.

Follow-up activities
* Record the new songs onto a cassette and let the children sing along with their own recordings.
* Make up songs to describe activities in which the whole group is taking part, for example (to the tune of 'The farmer's in his den') 'We all sit down to drink, we all sit down to drink, ee-eye-ee-eye, we all sit down to drink', thus reinforcing routine practice.
* Give the children musical instruments (or simple instruments made by the group) so that they can accompany their songs.

Links with home

Provide a short 'concert' for the adults, with the children singing their made-up songs.

Make a pattern

Learning outcome

To develop listening skills and the ability to recognise syllables within words.

Group size

Whole group.

What you need

Cassette recorder, cassette of nursery rhymes or familiar songs.

Preparation

Make sure that all the children are familiar with each other's names and with the names of the adults in the group.

What to do

Sit on the floor together, play the cassette and let the children sing along with the music. Suggest that you all clap to the rhythm of the songs, and begin with a simple tune. When the children know how to clap to the song, ask them to stand up and try stomping with their feet in time to the music, or slapping their hands on their thighs.

Sit down again and suggest that you try clapping each other's names. Begin with your own name. Say your name clearly, emphasising each syllable and clapping your hands for each one.

Then go round the circle, and ask each child to say their name and try to clap it. Let all the children clap the name together. When you've been all round the circle and each child has had a turn, play 'Who next?' – in this game you point to a particular child and everybody claps that child's name together.

Vary the game by clapping a child's name without saying it and asking the children to decide whose name it is.

At the end of the activity, encourage the children to explain to you in words what you have all been doing.

Questions to ask

Who's got the longest name? Who's got the shortest name? How many claps make (child's name)? Are any of the children's names the same when they are clapped? Are any nearly the same? What about when the names are spoken?

For younger children

Go over their names as often as necessary for them to understand the idea that one clap is equal to one sound or syllable. Any children who find the concept difficult to grasp will find it easier if you sit face to face with them, on a level, and encourage them to watch your mouth as you speak.

For older children

Let the children, in turns, lead the game of 'Who next?' and give what they think the clap is before the rest of the group.

Follow-up activities

* Teach the children the poem 'The engine driver' by Clive Sansom on photocopiable page 82.
* Sing familiar songs but miss out some of the words, clapping in the appropriate places. Ask the children to say the missing words.
* Vary the clapping by using musical instruments – you can make them with pot lids, wooden spoons, metal spoons, empty boxes, containers filled with rice and so on.
* Play a clapping game using different kinds of words. Think of a theme – animals, food, colours – tell the children the theme and ask them in turn to clap out words related to the theme for the rest of the group to guess.

Links with home

Encourage the children to explain in words what they have been doing in the activity. Can they clap out their names to someone at home?

Talking drums

Learning outcome

To develop listening skills and the ability to recognise syllables in words.

Group size

Large or small group.

What you need

A drum, or a box or pot that can be used as one.

What to do

Talk to the children about how words are made up of different sounds. Show them how to clap the pattern of their names, as in 'Make a pattern' on page 40. Then show them how they can clap the pattern of simple phrases or sentences, using one beat per syllable.

Sit the children in a circle with a good space between each child. The drum will be passed around the circle between them.

Choose a topic of conversation. It may be something that you have done together as a group, or a trip you have organised, or some other plans with which the children are familiar.

Begin yourself. Put the drum between you and the child next to you. If your subject is, for example, the trip you are going on, you might begin by beating the drum and saying the words at the same time.

'We are all going on a trip' (for this the beat would be * * * ** * * *).

Then the drum is passed along so that it is between the child next to you and the next child. The first child then continues the conversation and beats out his or her message at the same time:

'Where are we going?' (* * * **).

The drum is passed round again. The next child might say and beat out:

'We are going to the adventure playground' (* * ** * * *** **).

And so on.

Everyone should listen very carefully to both the message and the drumbeat. If the beat is right the child gets a round of applause.

Questions to ask

Does everyone know what we are going to talk about? Has everyone thought of something to say? Don't worry if somebody else says what you were going to say, you will probably think of something else when it comes to your turn. Are you all ready and waiting for your turn? How will you beat the drum?

For younger children

When doing this for the first time, try to do it in a small group of about four children because they may have difficulty keeping the timing right.

For older children

Let the children choose the topic of their conversation themselves, but make sure that it isn't something that isolates anyone or any part of the group.

Follow-up activities

* Do role-play activities in the same way, asking the children to tell the story of characters from nursery rhymes.
* Tell well-known stories, such as 'Goldilocks and the Three Bears', round the circle.
* Sing a song together, giving the children turns to beat out the rhythm on the drum.

Links with home

Encourage parents and carers to listen to and talk with the children and to hold prolonged conversations with them about different things.

Echoes

Learning outcome

To develop the ability to make up a story and speak with confidence.

Group size
Large or small group.

What you need
A beanbag or other small object.

What to do

Explain to the children what an echo is, that one voice repeats what the first one has said. Give them an example by saying something then repeating it. Say something again and ask the children to repeat it.

When the children have understood the idea, tell them that playing a game called 'Echoes' is a very good way to make up a story. Sit them in a circle and explain that each child is an 'Echo' of the child on their left. Begin to make up a story. You may give one or two sentences. For example, 'Once there was a star twinkling in the sky. But the star was sad because she really wanted to sparkle, not twinkle.'

When you are ready, pass the beanbag to the child on your left. That child has to echo the last bit of the story that you said, so he or she would say, 'She really wanted to sparkle, not twinkle' then add something of his or her own. The beanbag is then passed on to the next child for the echo to be said and the next part of the story to be added. And so on.

If any children want to add to part of the story out of turn, they should be given the chance, then the story goes back to where it left the circle and they still have a turn when the beanbag gets to them.

If the children run out of ideas, end the story and begin another one at the place where the beanbag is. (This means you need plenty of 'beginnings' under your belt!)

Questions to ask

How can we make our story exciting? How can we make it different? Who can think of some surprises to put into our story? Can we make our story last all the way round the circle? Can we give our story a happy ending?

For younger children

Keep the group quite small to begin with until the children have a good idea of what they have to do. Encourage the storytellers to speak clearly and with as much volume as they can, otherwise their 'Echoes' won't be able to hear them and they won't know what to say!

For older children

Keep the story going for as long as possible – challenge them to try to make the story last long enough to go round the circle twice.

Follow-up activities

* Ask the children to draw and colour pictures of their story and tell you what's happening in the pictures.
* Make a group 'big book' of the story, and suggest that the children do illustrations for it.
* Divide the children into two groups, each with a leader, and sing a song with one group leading and one group echoing just a line behind.

Links with home

Encourage the children to take their pictures home and tell their families all about the stories they have created together.

chapter six

Developing early reading skills

Learning to read is a continuous process that begins early. These activities will help children to develop an awareness of the written word and its everyday functions, to develop skills in recognising, matching and sequencing and to promote good attitudes to reading.

Shopping lists

Learning outcome

To match pictures, words and logos.

Group size

Two or three children.

What you need

Cut-out logos, pictures and words from old food packets and wrappers (for example, baked beans, chocolate bars, biscuits), card, PVA adhesive, felt-tipped pens.

Preparation

Stick the cut-out logos, pictures and words onto small pieces of card. If you have more than one of anything, so much the better.

What to do

Start by holding up each card and asking the children if they recognise any of the items shown. When they give you the correct word, write it on another small piece of card. Then hold up the word card at the same time as the picture card, displaying them side by side and pointing out the word.

Place all the cards, face up, in front of the children. Let them take turns to decide on items that will compile a group 'shopping list', each child choosing a card, for example beans, biscuits, iced cake. Then they should try to find the word which goes with their picture.

Questions to ask

Who goes shopping at home? What do you shop for? Who can see the 'beans' card? Who can see the 'biscuits' card? Can anybody tell me which card this one is? Can anybody see a card which is the same – which matches – this one?

For younger children

If you need to make the word cards simpler, draw the item from the picture card at the side of the printed word.

For older children

See if the children can recognise or 'read' any of the word cards first and then find the picture cards that go with them.

Follow-up activities

* Set up a group shop with empty packets and boxes, and take the children 'shopping' with card lists.
* Ask the children to describe their shopping trips to you.
* Play 'We went shopping and we bought...' in a circle. Each child tries to remember what went before and adds another item.

Links with home

Ask parents and carers to let the children find and identify appropriate goods on the shelves when they are shopping together.

What am I called?

Learning outcome

To recognise their own and each other's names.

Group size
Five or six children.

What you need
Card, scissors, felt-tipped pens.

Preparation
Print each child's name onto a piece of card about 20cm × 15cm.

What to do
Sit in a circle and hold up each name card in turn. Point out the beginning letter and its sound, run your finger along the name in a left to right direction and point out the ending sound. Can the children recognise any 'special' parts of the name, such as 'ch' or a double-letter sound? Tell them whose name it is and pass the card to that child, then go on to the next name.

When the children all have their name cards, play a game in which you ask for them back. Say, for example, 'I'm looking for a name that begins with a 't' sound'. When the card comes back to you, hold it up and say, 'Does this name begin with a 't' sound?' and then point out the features of the initial letter. You can make this part of the game more and more complicated as it progresses by asking, for instance, for a name with an 's' sound in the middle, or whatever is appropriate.

Then play a 'Who has the card for...?' game. Shuffle the cards and give them to the children at random. Then say, 'Who has the card for Rachel's name?', for example. When the child who has the card brings it back to you, go through all the features that make the card say Rachel's name.

Finally, hold up the cards and ask the children to call out the correct names, speaking together.

Questions to ask
Who knows what the sound is at the beginning of this name? Has anybody else got this sound in their name? Is the sound at the beginning or in the middle or at the end? Do we know what it looks like in the middle of your name instead of at the beginning? What is the difference?

For younger children
Keep the group small so that you don't confuse them with too many letters and words at once. Then gradually introduce more children to the group so that you have a greater variety of names, initials and sounds.

For older children
Before you start any of the games and activities, without doing any talking hold up the cards one by one and tell the children to put their hand up if the card shows their name.

Follow-up activities
* Paint self-portraits, then match name cards to the pictures.
* Make name badges to wear at the group.
* Help the children to trace, copy and write their own names in a variety of colours and with different writing implements.
* Read the poem 'Begins with "B"' by Gina Douthwaite on photocopiable page 79. Can the children guess the subject of the poem by looking at its shape on the page?

Links with home

Encourage the parents to take every opportunity to let the children read and write their names. Suggest that adults and children write short letters to each other that include their names.

Reading pictures

Learning outcome

To develop an understanding that pictures and words carry sequential meaning and move from left to right and from top to bottom.

Group size
Individuals.

What you need
Comics, scissors, paper, crayons.

Preparation
Cut out a simple sequence of pictures from a comic or make your own sequence of pictures. You need a sequence such as: child looking in shop window, child passing over money in exchange for toy, child playing with toy; or child with dog, child throws stick, dog chases stick, dog comes back with stick.

Make sure that your set of pictures has a very clear sequence that would not make sense if it was muddled up. Three pictures are enough to begin with. As the children's skills develop, you can make the sequences longer, say five pictures, then seven.

What to do
Show the child the three pictures in any order. Talk about each picture with the child, pointing out who is shown in each, and what is happening. Encourage the child to verbalise as much as possible.

Talk about the order in which the pictures appear. For instance, you might say, 'Could she play with the toy before she bought it?', 'Do you think she looked in the shop window to see the toy first?' and so on. This will give the child some clues about the order in which the pictures should be placed.

Now ask the child to put the pictures into an order that makes sense, beginning on the left-hand side. When the child can do this, suggest that he or she tells the story to you, beginning with the first picture and then moving from left to right.

Questions to ask
What's happening in this picture? Who is in the picture? What is she doing? Where is she? What do you think might happen next? Which picture do you think should come first? What happened first? Which picture do you think might be the last one? What happened in the end?

For younger children
Use pictures from comics that feature familiar characters and encourage the children to add as much information to the story as possible.

For older children
Ask the children to help you to add a few words underneath each picture. The cues they are given in the pictures will give them the confidence to try the words.

Follow-up activities
* Let the children make story scrap books by sticking chosen sets of pictures in sequence in a sugar-paper booklet.
* Draw illustrations of familiar nursery rhymes and use them for picture-sequencing activities.
* Collect a set of poster pictures for 'reading pictures' sessions with small groups.
* Cut out the pictures on photocopiable page 89 and ask the children to sequence them. Can they say the nursery rhyme 'Hey diddle diddle'?

Links with home

Give the children sets of pictures to take home and tell them to ask their parents or other adults to help them put the pictures in the right order.

Animal sounds

Learning outcome

To develop the ability to make sounds from recognition of a picture or shape.

Group size
Whole group.

What you need
Card, scissors, magazines (which contain pictures of animals), PVA adhesive, felt-tipped pens.

Preparation
Make some small cards, about 15cm × 12cm. Decide on a set of animals – this can be a mixture of domestic, farm and wild animals, such as:

budgie	pig	duck	mouse
dog	cow	owl	horse
cat	sheep	lion	bear

Draw one animal on each piece of card. Alternatively, you could cut animal pictures out of magazines and glue them onto the cards.

What to do
Teach the children the sounds that each animal makes, taking each card in turn and showing them the picture, telling them the name of the animal and making the sound. All the sounds are onomatopoeic – that is, they sound like the word. Ask the children to try to make the animal sounds themselves.

budgie	– tweet tweet
dog	– woof woof
cat	– miaow
mouse	– squeak squeak
pig	– oink oink
cow	– moo moo
sheep	– baa baa
horse	– neigh neigh
duck	– quack quack
owl	– toowittoowoo
lion	– roar
bear	– growl
fish	– pop pop pop

When the children know each sound, hold the cards up at random (without saying the animals' names) and ask them to make the correct sounds.

Questions to ask
Which animal is this? Does it fly? Does it swim? How many legs does it have? Where do you think it lives? Could you have one as a pet? What sound does it make?

For younger children
To begin with, keep your animals in separate groups of domestic, farm and wild and just do one or two animal cards at a time.

For older children
Tell them which groups are which, and where the animals live. Mix the groups up and ask them to tell you to which group the individual animals belong.

Follow-up activities
* Teach the children 'Old MacDonald had a farm', 'Hicketty Picketty, my black hen', 'Mary had a little lamb', 'Three blind mice' and 'Ding dong bell, pussy's in the well'.
* Look for pictures of animals to cut out and stick into an 'Animal book'.
* Play 'Collect the card' with small groups. The children take turns. You hold up a card and the child has to make the animal's sound. If it's correct he or she collects the card. The child with the most cards wins.
* Can the children say the sound of each animal on photocopiable page 90?

Links with home

Ask parents and carers to point out and talk about different animals and the sounds they make, when opportunities arise.

Signs and maps

Learning outcome

To develop sight recognition skills.

Group size
Two or three children to each adult.

What you need
Scissors, felt-tipped pens, card, plenty of adult help.

Preparation
Draw some large signs on pieces of card and cut them out. Make a mental note of different signs that you see during the day to give yourself ideas – these can be outside and inside. Outside you might find signs for a school crossing, a railway station, no right turn and so on. Inside you might find signs for cloakrooms, entrances and exits and so on.

Explain to parents that you will be taking the children out for a walk in the nearby vicinity, and ask for adult helpers to accompany the children.

What to do
Show the children the signs you have made and explain that they should look out for similar ones when they go out with you. Take them out for a walk, letting the children carry the signs themselves. Ask them to look out for signs they might recognise and then invite the children to match the signs to the cards. Explain what the signs mean if necessary.

When you return from your walk, ask the children if they can remember which signs they saw, where they saw them and what they meant. When they can recognise some of the signs, draw a simple map of the walk you took together. Draw the signs in the appropriate places. Ask the children if they can remember what they are.

Questions to ask
Have we seen this sign before? Do we have a sign the same as this? Is it a round sign, is it a square sign or is it another shape? What sound does the word begin with? Who can show us which way we went on the map? Who can see where our home is on the map? Can you see the sign which says...? Show me the way we walked.

For younger children
When the children are successful at matching the signs, see if they can recognise any of them and tell you what they stand for without any prompts or cues.

For older children
Encourage them to keep their own set of signs, and help you to draw the maps by telling you the route you took.

Follow-up activities
* Make a layout of the inside and outside environment, using cardboard packets and boxes as furniture or buildings and label the different places.
* With the children, draw an outline picture of your group's room, including the equipment and furniture, and show the children how such objects can be represented as shapes.
* Encourage the children to describe the layouts and maps in words.

Links with home

Ask parents and carers to help the children to notice signs and place-names on any journeys that they make, and to help them to copy signs and place-names to show to the group.

Let's match

Learning outcome

To develop the ability to match words to pictures.

Group size
Pairs.

What you need
Magazines and catalogues, card, paper, PVA adhesive, ruler, counters (in two different colours).

Preparation

Cut out two squares of card about 27cm square. Divide each card into nine equal small squares, three across and three down. One card will be the base card. Cut the other card into its nine small squares.

Cut out nine picture objects from the magazines or catalogues. Stick one picture to each small cut-out square. On the back of the square write what the object is (for example, bike, bird, cat). Write each of the words in one of the squares on your base card.

What to do

Give the counters to each pair of children, nine counters in one colour to one child, and nine in the other colour to the other child.

Show the children how to play the game. The individual cards should be placed in a pile, with the picture side up, or they can be spread out with the pictures showing. Two players take it in turns to take a card, decide what it is, turn it over and 'read' the word, then look for the word on the base card. When they get the right word they cover it up with their picture card. They then place one of their counters on their square. The aim is to get three counters in a row, up, down or across. If neither player gets a line, the cards are shuffled and play starts again.

When the children become familiar with the words, play the game with the words on the cards facing upwards (they can refer to the pictures to check if they have read the words correctly).

Questions to ask

Whose turn is it? Who will go first this time? What does the picture show? What sound does it begin with? What sound does it end with? Can you see a word that begins (and ends) with this sound? Do all the letters match?

For younger children

You could begin by matching picture to picture and having only the initial sound on the card instead of the word.

For older children

Make the game last longer by making a bigger board and dividing it into 12 or 16 squares. Let three children play instead of two (don't forget to have a third colour of counters!).

Follow-up activities

* Make catalogues by cutting out pictures from magazines, pasting them onto the pages of a booklet and labelling each picture. Help the children to 'read' the words.
* Collect posters and write labels for some of the items shown. Match the labels to the items in the pictures.
* Play games of 'Snap', matching a word with a picture instead of two pictures together.
* Complete the matching activity on photocopiable page 91.
* Read the poem 'Mouse' by Gina Douthwaite on photocopiable page 79, and let the children look at the layout of the poem.

Links with home

The children can be helped to label some of their special things at home. They will soon learn to recognise the words.

Match the words

Learning outcome

To develop the ability to match a written word with a spoken word.

Group size
Whole group.

What you need
Card, felt-tipped pens, scissors.

Preparation
Make some large cards and on each card write a movement word:

jump	run	wobble
hop	stand	creep
skip	shake	slither

What to do
Show the children about three words at a time. Try to make sure that they begin and end with different letters. For instance, you could show them 'jump', 'hop' and 'wobble'. When you show them the words, spend plenty of time on each one, saying the word, pointing with your finger in a left to right direction from the beginning of the word to the end of it and pointing out the beginning sound and the ending sound. Tell the children to copy the sounds you make and say the word as you point to it.

All the children should sit in a circle. Place three word cards face down in the centre of the circle. Choose one child to take a card. Ask the child to try to read the word on the card and then give it to you. Hold up the card for all the children to see. The child who took the card should then say the word and do the action. If the other children think he or she is doing the right action they can join in. If they think the child is wrong they should sit still and the child can have another go, with everyone helping by saying the beginning sound and the end-sound of the word.

For younger children
Begin and end each session with a recap of what each word says, showing the children the direction in which the word is read, and pointing out the beginning and the ending sounds.

For older children
Add more words as you go along. You will have to recall previous words that have been used but they will be able to cope with more and more words for each session. Try adding one new word first, then two.

Questions to ask
What letter is this? What sound does this letter make? What sound is at the beginning of the word? What sound is at the end of the word? Who can tell me what the word says? Which word says 'jump'? Which word says 'hop'? Which word says 'wobble'?

Follow-up activities
* Play 'Pick the word'. Let the children take turns to choose which action they want to do, then take the word card that goes with it.
* Play 'Find the word' with a group of three or four children. Turn all the word cards face down. One child chooses a word, says it out loud, then the other children take turns to turn over one word at a time. If they turn over the right word they keep it. If it is not the right word it is turned back again. The child with the most words is the winner.

Links with home

Send sentences home that include movement words, such as 'Lucy can skip', and ask parents or other adults to read them with the children.

Letter match

Learning outcome

To develop the ability to match written letters.

Group size

Three or four children.

What you need

Card, felt-tipped pens.

Preparation

Make two sets of alphabet cards by cutting out 26 small pieces of card for each set – the cards should be easy to handle. Write the alphabet on the cards ('a' on one card, 'b' on the next and so on).

What to do

Shuffle both sets of cards. Put one set of cards in a pile, with the letters facing downwards. Deal four cards from the other set to each player.

Turn over the top card of the full set and place it at the side of the pile so that it is facing the children the right way up. Explain to the children that they should take turns to look at their set of four cards to see if they have a matching card. If they do, they can take the card to make a pair and are given another card from the remains of the set that has been dealt out. They should then put their pair to one side.

If no one can match the letter, the card remains at the side of the first pile and another card is turned over; when there are no more cards left to turn over, these cards are shuffled and used again.

Continue with the game until all the pairs are collected. The child who has the most pairs is the winner.

Questions to ask

Who's going first? Whose turn is next? Does anybody know which letter we're looking for? What sound does it make? Do you know any words beginning with the sound? Do you know any words ending with the sound? Does this letter begin anybody's name?

For younger children

Let the children spread their set of six cards out in front of them so that they can see them easily. Help them by making sure that all their cards are the right way up.

For older children

Encourage them to name the letter that is turned over each time.

Follow-up activities

* Play 'Letter snap' with the cards.
* Help the children to put the cards into alphabetical order, using an alphabet frieze as a model.
* Go through the cards, asking the children to name something that begins with each letter as you hold it up.
* Make up alliterative sentences with the children. For example, if the letter 'j' has been chosen, say 'Jack jigged and jogged jollily'.
* Read the story 'Pots and tripes' on photocopiable page 84.

Links with home

Choose a different letter for each week. Parents can help the children to identify things that begin with that letter. They can then relate how many things they have seen beginning with a specific sound.

Word for word

Learning outcome

To develop the ability to match words.

Group size
Two or three children.

What you need
Sugar paper, Sellotape, card, scissors, felt-tipped pens.

Preparation
Make a little dictionary of words that the children use frequently. These could be names, family words and group words such as 'toys', 'sand', 'pencils' and so on.

To make the dictionary cut the sugar paper in half, fold it in half again and then put the folded sheets together to form a 'book'. This can be stapled in the centre or tied.

Draw a line down the middle of each page. On the right-hand side of the page make three pockets by cutting out small pieces of sugar paper and Sellotaping them to the pages. On the left-hand side of the page write three words down the page. Copy the same words onto small pieces of card that will fit into the pockets.

What to do
Place all the words face upwards on a table, with the children around them. Open the dictionary at the first page Explain to the children that, together, you are going to put the words in the right pockets.

Read the first word to them. Point out which letter it begins with. Show them how the word reads from left to right. Give them time to look through the words laid out on the table and find the word that is exactly the same. When they have found it, place it in its pocket and go on to the next word.

When all the words are in their pockets, go back to the beginning and see if any of the children can remember what any of the words say.

Questions to ask
Is it a long word or a short word? What kind of shape is this word? What does the word mean? What sound does it begin with? What sound does it end with? Can we find any words that begin with the same sound? Do all the letters match the letters in the word or only some of them? Which letters match? Which letters don't match?

For younger children
Start with only a few words; six spread over two pages would be ample. Repeat the game several times so that they are given the chance to remember the auditory and visual clues.

For older children
Add new words for each session. Help them to read through all the words on the pages and then all the words on the table before they begin to match them.

Follow-up activities
* Make a dictionary of words from nursery rhymes and help the children to learn the nursery rhymes and the words at the same time.
* Make a dictionary in the same way but put pictures on the pockets to help the children recognise what the words say as a first step to reading them.
* Make word cards in sets of two and play 'Word snap'.

Links with home

Make 'word envelopes', containing words that individual children can recognise, to send home. Ask parents to listen to the children practising the words that they have learned.

I can...

Learning outcome

To develop the ability to match the shape of a letter with the sound it makes.

Group size
Large or small groups.

What you need
Card, felt-tipped pens, scissors, PVA adhesive.

Preparation
Prepare some letter cards by cutting out some large blank cards and printing a lower case letter on each.

What to do
Explain to the children that you are going to work on sounds that letters make. Choose a letter you are going to work on. It is much more important for the children to learn the sound of the letter rather than the name, though you can make a passing reference to the letter's name.

With all the children sitting down, hold up the card with the letter on it. Tell them the sound that the letter makes and show them the shape of the letter by tracing it with your finger from top to bottom, in the way you would write it. Invite them to trace the shape of the letter in the air, saying its sound.

Explain to the children that they are going to think of things they can do which begin with the sound of the letter. For instance, if the letter is 'b' they might say, 'I can bend my leg', 'I can bark', 'I can blow bubbles' and so on.

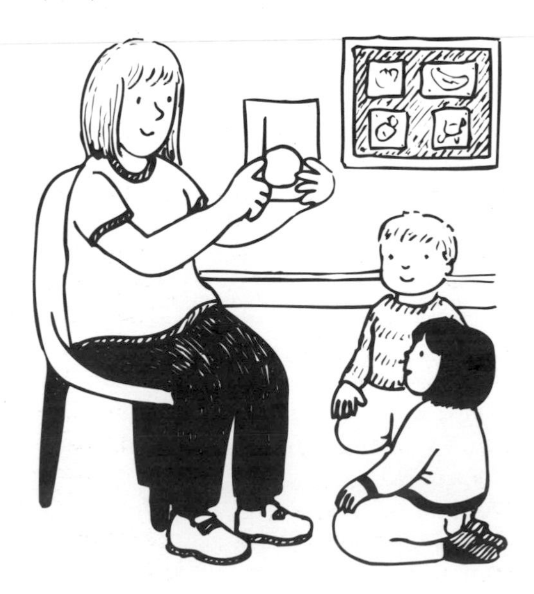

Concentrate on one letter at a time, then when the children have done as much as they can with the letter, end the session rather than introduce another sound. Save new sounds for different sessions.

Questions to ask
Whose name begins with this letter? Can you see anything in the room that begins with this sound? Do you know any more words with this sound in it?

For younger children
It is sometimes quite difficult for younger children to hear a sound in isolation because consonants are always followed by vowel sounds, for example the 'b' in 'baby' is followed by the sound 'ay', so they might understand 'bay' but not 'b'. You may need to give them a little help, such as telling them that the sound 'b' is at the beginning of the word 'bend'.

For older children
Extend the activity by asking them to think of something they can eat or drink that begins with the sound you are working on.

Follow-up activities
* See if the children can look through books and comics to spot the letter that has been the focus of the activity.
* Make a poster of the children's names, showing their initial letters as capitals and lower case letters side by side.
* Play 'I can see', giving the children the beginning sounds of the words, that is, the consonant and its following vowel sound – 'it begins with tay' for table, 'it begins with 'peh' for pencil, and so on.
* Photocopiable page 92 focuses on the letter 's'. Ask the children to name the objects before completing the sheet.
* Read the poem 'Hissssss' on photocopiable page 82.

Links with home

Ask parents and other adults at home to play lots of 'I spy' games with the children to help reinforce knowledge of letter sounds.

chapter seven

Sharing books

When you are sharing books in an enjoyable way the children see them as a source of pleasure, as well as information, and it gives them the motivation to want to learn to read. The activities in this chapter provide many different starting points for sharing books.

In the right order

Learning outcome

To develop sequencing skills.

Group size

Two or three children at a time.

What you need

A known book, or the story 'Pots and tripes' on photocopiable page 84, paper, felt-tipped pens.

What to do

Read the story with the children. Your aim in this activity is to encourage them to pick out the main features of the story, and you can help them by asking: who is in the story? Who else is in the story? What does (first character) do? What does (second character) do? What do (other characters) do?

On each sheet of paper draw and write each of these features. For instance, if you were working on the story 'Pots and tripes', you would pick out Susie S going to bed, Mister M doing his decorating, the wallpaper as it should have been and as it was, and so on.

Let the children colour in your pictures and dictate words to you to accompany them so that they are really involved in the story.

When the sheets are finished, shuffle them and then suggest that the children put them into the right order. Make sure that they do their sequencing from left to right and then go back to the beginning of the line for the next row of sheets.

For younger children

Three or four pages will be plenty to begin with so confine the sequencing activity to the most simple elements of the story.

For older children

As the children mature and develop their abilities, you can go into greater detail and add more and more pages.

Follow-up activities

* Use the completed sequencing sheets to make a book.
* Organise different sequencing activities – pattern sequencing, bead-threading sequencing, word sequencing and so on.
* With emergent readers use sentence-sequencing activities, writing the words on cards and asking the children to place them in the correct order.
* Make sets of sequencing cards for some well-known and favourite stories, such as *The Very Hungry Caterpillar* by Eric Carle (Puffin) and *Rosie's Walk* by Pat Hutchins (Puffin).

Links with home

Send sets of sequencing cards home for the children to place in the correct order. Ask parents and other adults to help the children to retell the known stories in their correct sequence.

Build a book corner

Learning outcome

To develop a firm interest in all kinds of books and to take part in developing the book corner.

Group size
Whole group.

What you need
As many book resources as you can gather together, some kind of book shelving, display resources (such as a table).

Preparation
Choosing books for the children is a very important task. There needs to be a selection of books which suit all of the children's present level of development. You should provide board books with pictures and no text, books where the story is shown in pictures and where the text is very short, books with more complex pictures and text, and home-made books which you have put together with the children.

What to do
Share the books with the children. Try to stimulate their individual attention, self-esteem and confidence by:

* looking for books that reflect their interests and experiences;
* providing books that show real children in a real world, so that they can 'identify' with the people in the books;
* searching out books that show people of all races, abilities and social groups;
* providing dual-language books to develop an awareness that English is not the only language in which books are written;
* giving the children plenty of opportunities for interaction by providing flap books, pop-up books and books with questions to answer;
* encouraging the children to use a selection of reference books so that they can recognise that a book doesn't necessarily mean a story or a poem.

Keep the book corner in a light and airy place and provide beanbags, cushions, mats and armchairs (if possible) for the children to sit on. Display the books so that they are all within easy reach, with the front covers being clearly visible.

Questions to ask
Do the children take good care of the books? What 'rules' can we apply to the book corner to assure the books of a good, long shelf-life? Are the displays changed regularly to keep interest from waning and do they provide challenges?

For younger children
Encourage them to enjoy sharing the books with other children and other adults by 'reading' them together, retelling the stories or poems to each other and discussing them.

For older children
Help the children to develop their own reasons for choices – 'I want to read this book because the pictures look good'; 'I want to read this book because I've read one about this character before and I like him'; 'I want to read this book because it's new to me and looks exciting' and so on.

Links with home

Send books home for sharing. This reinforces the idea that if children enjoy books they will become motivated to learn to read later on and this will lay the foundation required for reading skills.

Follow-up activities
* Share regular reading times together, and let the children 'read' together in pairs.
* Make books of the children's favourite stories and characters.

Be a storyteller

Learning outcome

To participate in the reading of stories.

Group size
Any number of children.

What you need
Picture story books with strong, repetitive and predictable language, such as 'Goldilocks and the Three Bears', 'The House that Jack Built' and 'The Billy Goats Gruff'.

What to do
Read the picture book several times, sometimes drawing your finger along the words you are reading to reinforce the direction in which the words are read. Emphasise the rhythm and the rhymes and let the children join in, where appropriate. The strong, repetitive language in traditional stories such as 'Goldilocks and the Three Bears' provides many opportunities for audience participation.

Once the children know the story, it can be repeated at any time and they will be able to respond to it. The fun of the stories is in their consistent repetition. If you stray from the storyline they will notice the alteration. If you pause before a known part of the text (for example, 'Who's been eating *my* porridge?') they will be able to fill in the gap for you.

Questions to ask
What is this book about? Who can remember what (name of character) said when (describe event)? Who thinks (name of character) was right to do (describe event)? Who thinks (name of character) was wrong to (describe event)? Why? Which is your favourite part of the story? What do you like best about the book?

For younger children
Think ahead about specific actions that the children can learn to do, and appropriate sounds, words or phrases that they can say at various points in the story. Carry out the actions and say the words yourself when you reach the parts of the story in which they occur. The children will quickly pick up on the idea that they can do these too.

For older children
Give individual children the opportunity to be the storyteller with you, holding up the book, telling the story and letting the other children join in where appropriate.

Follow-up activities
* Paint pictures to illustrate specific sections of favourite stories. Display them together with the words that are spoken by the children when they join in with the storyteller. For example, pictures of Daddy Bear trying out his chair could be accompanied by the words 'Daddy Bear said, 'Who's been sitting in *my* chair?'
* Write your own stories and include small sections that encourage the children to join in. Base them on known stories, but use the children as characters. For example, take *Brown Bear, Brown Bear, What Do You See?* by Bill Martin (Picture Puffin), replacing words from the book with 'Sophie, Sophie, what can you do?'
* Act out the stories in short drama sessions.
* Read the story 'The alphabet hunt' by Karen King on photocopiable page 85 to the children.

Links with home

Organise a storytelling session and demonstrate how stories and poems can be made to 'come alive' for the children.

Exploring books

Learning outcome

To develop a positive attitude towards books and reading and to learn 'book' vocabulary.

Group size
Three or four children.

What you need
A box of different kinds of books.

What to do
Sit with the children and browse through the books with them. Let them get used to handling the books themselves if they are unfamiliar with them. Talk about the different kinds of books that are in the box. Some may be story books, some may be reference books. You can also add poetry or nursery rhyme books to the set. Say, for example, 'Look, this books tells us the story of The Gingerbread Man,' or 'Look, this book tells us all about things with wheels,' or 'Let's see if we can find a book with a story about a dinosaur.' Gradually the children will come to understand that books have different purposes.

While you are looking at the books with the children, use 'book vocabulary' such as 'Let's look at the cover to see what it's called,' and 'Which is the first page?' and help the children to go through the pages one by one, so that they understand how the book 'works'.

Show them how the print runs from left to right, and how when you get to the end of one line you go back to the beginning of the next. Talk about words – for example, 'Which word do you think says gingerbread?' – running your finger along the word to reinforce the concept of a word being a group of letters.

Point to the pictures in the book and read the appropriate text to reinforce the idea that the words are relevant to the illustrations.

For younger children
Keep the sessions short so that they are within the children's attention span and make sure that the books you are showing them are appropriate to their stage of development. Don't labour the point of the 'book' vocabulary, but remember that you are acting as a role model and the children will take their lead from you and begin to learn the appropriate language.

For older children
Even for readers or emergent readers the book-sharing experience is a crucial part of their literacy development. They will still enjoy you reading to them, particularly much-loved texts, and will enjoy being involved with other children in the group. Your support and enjoyment will help them to develop good attitudes towards literacy.

Follow-up activities
* Seek out books in other languages and share them with the children.
* Make booklets out of coloured paper and help the children to create their own illustrated stories. Don't worry if they only scribble at this stage – it is the physical process of making the book that is important. Give their books as much credibility as published books and discuss the cover, the pages, the words and the pictures.
* Use appropriate books to prepare the children for events that are going to happen in the group, for example a trip to a particular place, a visit from the police or the fire service or someone going to hospital.

Links with home

Plan a session in which you show parents how you involve the children with books, encouraging them to do the same at home. Or you may wish to send home the letter on photocopiable page 76.

Writing a book

Learning outcome

To make up and write books using specified vocabulary.

Group size
Two or three children.

What you need
Paper, black marker pen, scissors, card, ribbon or wool, hole punch, PVA adhesive, crayons.

What to do
Decide on the specific vocabulary goal that you are aiming at – for example, you might want to teach the children the word 'inside'. Tell the children that together you are going to make a book that uses the word 'inside'. Give the children a sentence as an example for the first page. You might say, 'Our first page says: when it rains all the children go *inside* the house.' Ask them if they think that's a good first page. If they agree with your sentence, write the words carefully on the page, leaving space for a picture.

Encourage the children to give you the words for subsequent pages. They might suggest things like: the biscuits are *inside* the box; the beans are *inside* the tin; the cars are *inside* the garage; the books are *inside* the cupboard.

Work on about five or six pages per book. Keep the pages simple so that your vocabulary goal doesn't get lost in a clutter of words. Try to have a surprise ending on the last page, which could introduce a different word. In this example you might write, as the last page: the sun comes out and we all go *outside* to play.

Read the words slowly to the children as you write them. When the text for the book has been written, ask the children to do illustrations for each page, then cut them out and glue them in the book. Use two sheets of card as front and back covers, and tie the book together with ribbon or wool. Give it a title and write the children's names on the front cover as authors.

Questions to ask
While you are writing: who can think of something else that is *inside* something? Do you have another example? What else can we write about?

When the book has been put together: who remembers what the first page says? Who remembers what this page says? and so on. Who can find the word 'inside' on this page? Who can find the word 'outside'?

For younger children
The vocabulary goals need not necessarily be new words or phrases. If they are words and phrases that the children use in their speech they will also learn to identify them on paper as you make the book together.

For older children
As you fill the pages write the vocabulary goal word or phrase in pencil and give the children opportunities to trace over it for you.

Follow-up activities
* Read the books together, often, as a group and with individual children, so that they learn and remember the words.
* Encourage the children to 'read' the books to other members of the group and other adults.
* Write stories following traditional patterns, such as 'The Enormous Turnip', using specific vocabulary goals.

Links with home

Let the children take the books home to share with their families and friends. Keep a 'library list' and let the children write in their names as they take the books and tick them off as they bring them back.

What's next?

Learning outcome

To develop the ability to predict what might happen next.

Group size
Any number of children.

What you need
A selection of story books (some of these should be new to the children).

What to do

Find a place where the children can sit in comfort to share the books with you. Read a familiar story to them, stopping in different places to pause and giving the children the chance to fill in the words. If the story is really well known to them you may be able to read one page or spread and the children the next. This will give them the idea of taking turns in the 'reading'.

Then introduce the children to a new story book, show them the cover, and flick through some of the picture pages to whet their appetite. Ask them what they think the story is about, from the pictures. What do they think might happen in the story?

Begin to read the story. At certain points pause and ask the children what they think might happen next. They might be able to give you certain words that they anticipate, or the next event in the story. Ask them why they think that will happen.

Go on to the next part of the story, and then stop and recap whether it was what they expected or whether it was a surprise. Read the story to the end.

Questions to ask

Were there any surprises in the story? Did you think it would end like that? Was it a good ending? Can you think of any other ways it might have ended? Why didn't it end in those ways? What bit of the story did you like best? Why?

For younger children

Give the children plenty of time to think about what they want to say and then verbalise it. It sometimes helps to point to the pictures to give them clues.

For older children

Give them opportunities to respond and discuss together what they think will happen next, then gather all their information together and say 'So we think... Let's go on to the next bit and see if we're right, shall we?'

Follow-up activities

* Talk about what the children thought might happen in the story, what led them to think that, and what really happened. How satisfied are they with what happened?
* Ask the children to draw and 'write' the new story, to take home.
* Tape-record the children telling their versions of the story.
* Make a poster that focuses on the first part of the story. Ask individual children to dictate to you what they thought would happen at a particular point. For example, 'Jo thought this would happen...' Then write what actually happened in the story: 'This is what really happened...'

Links with home

Ask the children to show the poster to their parents and to point out which section of the poster was their contribution. Encourage them to talk through their ideas with the adults.

The house that Jack built

Learning outcome

To make a group book using a familiar story as a model.

Group size
Small numbers of children at a time (ideally, the book should belong to the whole group).

What you need
Photocopiable pages 80–81, sugar paper, hole punch, ribbon or wool, pencils, felt-tipped pens, paints, PVA adhesive, scissors.

What to do
Read 'The house that Jack built' on photocopiable pages 80–81 several times; the children will soon learn to join in and to anticipate what's coming next in the rhyme.

Tell the children that they are going to make their own book about 'The house that Jack built'. Talk about the story – what are the important parts that they will need to include? How can they make the story into a book? Talk about the pages in a book and how two pages that face each other are called a 'double-page spread'.

Cut your sugar paper to an appropriate size, fold it in half and count the double-page spreads together. You will need a spread for each stanza of the rhyme, that is each time a new item or character is introduced. So the first double-page spread will be for 'This is the house that Jack built', the second will be for 'This is the malt that lay in the house...' and so on. When you have established how many spreads will be required, fix the sheets together to make a book.

Let the children draw or paint pictures relevant to the story, and help them to cut them out to make smaller pictures that can be used in the book. Print the words on the left-hand page of the spread. The children's pictures can then be pasted onto the right-hand page of the spread.

Write the title of the book 'The house that Jack built' on the front cover and add the children's names as authors. (Laminate the book if you wish to make it more durable.) Finally, share the book with the children.

Questions to ask
Who knows what this page says? Can anyone recognise this word? Who wants to read the story out? What pictures do we need? How many pictures have we got on this page? Which is your favourite page? Which bit do you like saying best? Why?

For younger children
Help them to draw the outline of appropriate illustrations for the pages and then they can colour them in.

For older children
The children will be able to draw, colour, cut and stick their own pictures, with guidance to make sure that they are working on the correct page or are not encroaching on anyone else's pictures when they are pasting.

Follow-up activities
* Make other group books of well-known nursery rhymes.
* Let the children have access to the book to read and share as often as they wish.
* Talk about how you made the book together; can the children remember the sequence you worked in?
* Help the children to 'read' the words of their book by drawing your finger along them as the children tell you the story from memory.

Links with home

Let the children take turns to take the book home for sharing. Alternatively, invite parents or other adults into the group to read to the children sometimes.

A week on a book

Learning outcome

To understand how stories are made up and how print works.

Group size

Three or four children at a time.

What you need

A book with a strong repetitive text, chosen specifically for the week, for example *Brown Bear, Brown Bear, What Do You See?* by Bill Martin (Picture Puffin).

Preparation

Read the book to yourself, noting any special features in it – for instance, the rhyme, the rhythm, who the characters are, which elements are repetitive. This will help you to plan the whole week's activities.

Plan the schedule of activities. For example, on Monday read the book. On Tuesday re-read the book and do some drama and movement work for the story. On Wednesday make simple stick puppets of the main character. On Thursday re-create the book together (see the previous activity). On Friday create an alternative story, using the story pattern but substituting characters and events, for example if you were using *Brown Bear, Brown Bear*, create a story that says: '(child's name, child's name) what do you see? I see a (child's choice) looking at me!'

What to do

First, talk about the book's cover and ask the children what they think the book will be about. Does the cover support their ideas?

Read the story with lots of enthusiasm, pointing to the words as you read. Stop occasionally to ask the children to predict what might happen next but don't question them too much. Read the story again, encouraging the children to follow and join in as you point to the words. Elicit the children's responses to the story – which bit did they like best?

Put the rest of the week's planned schedule of activities into operation.

Questions to ask

What happened? What might happen next? What would you like to happen next? Can you join in with this part? Can you remember what comes on the next page? Can you read this page with me?

For younger children

Re-read the book as many times as the children will listen to it, but try to vary the ways in which the children participate – sometimes by predicting, sometimes by responding to the text, sometimes by remembering the sequencing.

For older children

Try using a kind of oral 'cloze' procedure, where you read part of a text but omit a key word or phrase, asking the children to provide it.

Follow-up activities

* Use sugar paper to make a 'big book' of the story, keeping to the text as much as possible.
* Act out the story in small groups.
* Clap the pattern of the repeating phrases, together.
* Help the children to do illustrations of their favourite parts of the story. This will help to bring meaning to the print and enable them to understand the structure of the story.

Links with home

Let the children take turns to take the book home and share it with their family.

Help with the story

Learning outcome

To develop an interest and response to books.

Group size
Small groups at a time.

What you need
A book that you have chosen, a board, card, black marker pen, felt-tipped pens, crayons, scissors, Blu-Tack.

Preparation
After reading through your chosen book, pick out the characters and any key objects that appear in the story. Select key words that the children will remember from the text. List the characters, objects and words, and then make some blank cards – 15cm × 15cm for the characters and objects, and 15cm × 10cm for the words.

What to do
Read the story to the children, telling them that you are going to make a set of characters, objects and words and then use the sets to tell the story on a storyboard. Ask them to tell you all the characters. Draw the characters on the pieces of card as they offer them. Let the children colour them in. You may want to write the name of the character at the bottom of each card. Do the same with the objects.

Ask the children if they can remember any of the words that they think are important to the story. Write each word on one of the blank word cards and read them out. Check against your list that nothing important has been left out, and fix Blu-Tack to the back of each card.

Sit in a circle, and hand out the cards to individual children, making sure they know what their card is. Read the story again. At each point when one of the characters, objects or words is mentioned or becomes involved in the story, invite the child who holds the appropriate card to come up and place it on the storyboard. Move the characters around on the board as the story develops.

Store the cards in a box close to the book for when it is read again.

Questions to ask
Who was in the story? Was there anyone else? What happened in the story? Which do you think are important words in the story? What was the story about?

For younger children
When they are sitting in the circle, you might have to remind them which card they have been given. Encourage them to bring their card up to the front of the group and fix it on the board.

For older children
Don't be afraid to use the technical vocabulary such as 'character', 'event' and 'object'. Encourage the children to tell the story in pairs, one 'reading', the other using the cards to tell it on the storyboard.

Follow-up activities
* See if the children can tell the story to you, when they've heard it a few times, with you placing the cards on the storyboard.
* Tape-record the story so that they can use the cards with a cassette version, perhaps checking with the book as they listen to it.
* Suggest that the children choose more books with which they would like to do this activity.
* Ask the children to respond to photocopiable page 93, 'Make a story'.

Links with home

Let the children take turns to use the cards at home to help them to retell the story to members of their family and friends.

The riches of reading

Learning outcome

To learn that books offer opportunities to experience objects, actions and events.

Group size

Any number of children.

What you need

A selection of different kinds of books – flap books, books without text, pop-up books, picture story books and so on.

What to do

Sitting in a comfortable place with the children, look at the books together. Talk about the format of the books – how the pages work, how the writing is presented. Look closely at the pictures and talk about special features, such as pop-ups and flaps. Discuss the ideas that are conveyed by the text. Encourage the children to respond to the books and verbalise their own ideas. Give them as much time as they need to formulate their responses.

When you share books together you are encouraging the development of communication and the development of good literacy skills by:

* developing the children's concentration and attention span;
* showing your own interested involvement, which will encourage a positive attitude towards books and learning to read;
* helping them to imitate language, label objects and expand conversation, and to discuss what is happening in the books;
* helping them to develop the ability to take turns naturally;
* reinforcing new language and concepts by reading and re-reading favourites;
* focusing on different words and ideas, which the children will feel encouraged to explain.

Questions to ask

Which book do you like best? Why do you like it? What is the best bit about it? Can we find any more books like this one? What can you see in this picture? What do you think is happening here? Who is this story about? Do you know any more stories about this character?

For younger children

Try to include as much one-to-one sharing of books as you can, but also encourage them to have one-to-one book sharing with other children; leave them to their own devices, but 'eavesdrop' to see how they're getting on from time to time!

For older children

Help them to develop the skill of 'browsing' through the books in order to make their own choice of books they would like to share. Help them to organise their ideas: do they like books with lots of pictures in them? Do they like books with the same characters? What about trying something completely different?

Follow-up activities

* Learn the song 'Tell me a story, little book' on photocopiable page 86.
* Encourage the children to bring books from home to share with the group as well as sending books home for the children to share with their families.
* Have a 'Choice of the week'. Nominate someone at the beginning of the week to choose their special interest book for everyone else to share, and put it on display with a notice saying 'Indra's favourite book this week is...'.
* Have special 'sharing books' times as part of your routine.

Links with home

Take every opportunity to encourage family members to share books with the children. Explain the importance of an early start and that their role is crucial in showing children that books are enjoyable and fun.

chapter eight

Early writing skills

As with reading, writing is a skill that needs much motivation. You will play a crucial part in the learning process because if you can engender a positive attitude towards writing from these very early days, children will always associate the activity with enjoyment. These activities are designed to help children to learn pencil control, while still being good fun.

Pictures and sounds

Learning outcome

To remember a shape and then form it.

Group size

Two or three children.

What you need

A large sheet of card or paper for each child, felt-tipped pens, pencils, crayons, scissors.

Preparation

Fold each child's sheet of paper in half.

What to do

Let the children take turns to choose something to draw. Suppose a child would like to draw a butterfly. On the front of the paper draw a simple butterfly. Give it a body and two wings and a little head and, perhaps, a simple symmetrical pattern on the wings. Talk through the drawing as you are doing it, naming the different parts of the butterfly and the different shapes you are drawing. Now unfold the page. On the inside begin to draw another butterfly but omit some of the detail.

The task for the child is to look at the first drawing, look at the second, remember what is missing and try to draw it to complete the picture.

Now do the same with a letter. Ask the child what sound the word 'butterfly' begins with; draw a 'b' on the top sheet and part of a 'b' on the inside. Ask the child to look, remember, say the sound and complete the letter.

Questions to ask

Watch how I draw this – where did I start? How many shapes can you see? What are they? Which bit have I missed? What shape is it? Can you do it?

For younger children

The children may find it more difficult to remember what's missing, carry that shape in their head when they turn to the inside of the paper, then work out where it goes and how to draw it. Therefore keep the pictures as simple as you can.

For older children

Work on capital letters as well, explaining to the children that a capital letter is used for the beginning of their names.

Follow-up activities

* Play 'Guess the letter' where you draw part of a letter and the children finish it. Can they name the letter?
* Help the children to draw sets of different shapes, and sets of letters.
* Do potato prints of shapes and letters – this will show them that they can be repeated over and over again and that writing involves repetition.
* The completion of photocopiable page 92 will reinforce knowledge of the letter 's'.

Links with home

Send some of the children's work home, encouraging the children to tell their family members about how they have been learning to remember different shapes and letters.

Fit the word

Learning outcome

To use familiar words and letters to label a picture.

Group size
Two or three children.

What you need
A poster showing a large picture (on any subject relevant to the children's interests), a black marker pen, paper, pencils, crayons, felt-tipped pens, scissors, PVA adhesive.

What to do
Show the children your chosen poster, pointing out interesting items and encouraging them to tell you everything that they can see in it. Is there anything happening in the picture?

Suggest that, together, you make a set of labels for the picture and display it. Talk through the picture, asking the children which things they might make labels for – if it was a parkland scene you might label flowers, a tree, a dog, a buggy, a slide, swings and so on.

Do one word at a time, writing the word on a piece of paper to show them which letters it has and what it looks like. Give each child a turn to 'write' a word. Let the child whose turn it is choose whether to trace over your word, copy it or let you help to guide the writing implement, and respond appropriately. As you are writing each word make the sounds very carefully and show the children how it is read from left to right.

Display the poster where the children choose. Go through the labels with the children, fixing them onto the poster in the appropriate places.

Questions to ask
What sound does our word begin with? Does anybody know what that letter looks like? Can you trace the letter in the air with your finger? What other sounds are in the word?

For younger children
It might help to draw a little picture symbol at the beginning of each label to help them to recognise the word later when you have mounted the display.

For older children
As well as single words, write one or two phrases or sentences, for example 'The boys are at the park' and help them to have a go at reading them.

Follow-up activities
* Play a game in which you take the poster down, remove its labels then the children have to read the labels and put them in the relevant places (you can do this on a table).
* Use several different posters, framing the word labels in different colours to make it easier to identify which set of words goes with which poster.
* Encourage lots of bead threading and pegboard work to assist the development of fine motor control.

Links with home

Show the children's labelled poster to parents and ask them to try to take the opportunity to do something similar at home, perhaps with a poster in the child's bedroom.

Magic stepping stones

Learning outcome

To practise writing own names with appropriate use of upper and lower case letters.

Group size
Five or six children.

What you need
A large space, card, pencils, crayons, felt-tipped pens, scissors.

Preparation
Cut the card into lots of pieces; each one will be a stepping stone. Work out how many stepping stones you will need to get from one side of the room to the other with only small spaces in between. If you are working on shapes you can cut the card into the shapes that the children are learning.

What to do
Explain to the children that you are going to play a game called 'Magic stepping stones' in which they start at one side of the room and can only get to the other side by stepping on stones. But the stones only work if they have somebody's name written on them. So all the children will need to write their name on a stepping stone.

Work at each child's level of development to help them to write their names. Some will need help in holding the writing implement with you guiding them, some will be able to trace over your writing, some may be able to copy their name after you have written it, and some may be able to write their name by themselves.

When all the names have been written, set the stepping stones in a path along the floor. You may need to wait until several small groups have completed their name-writing.

The children should then take turns to step across the stones with you calling out the names, 'Step to Lisa's stone, now step to Matthew's stone' and so on. Encourage the children to recognise the names and join in with the calling out of them.

Questions to ask
Have we got a stepping stone for everyone? Who is missing? Whose name is this? How many stepping stones do we need? Who knows what sound this name begins with? Whose name might it be? Can anyone write their name all by themselves?

For younger children
Make sure that there is plenty of space on the pieces of card for the children to write their names, and provide large, fat writing implements for an easy grip.

For older children
If they can manage to write their names carefully by themselves, draw a line on the card and let them try to write on the line.

Links with home

When you write letters home, give the children opportunities to write their own names on them.

Follow-up activities

* Practise writing names on paintings, books and so on.
* Cut out letters from different materials, such as sandpaper or textured wallpaper, and encourage the children to trace the letters with their fingers to get the feel of the shape of each letter. Help them to glue their names, made from these letters, onto card.
* Cut out stencil shapes of the letters of their names and let them colour them.

Washing lines

Learning outcome

To learn different letters and to practise writing them.

Group size
Three or four children.

What you need
A large space, paper or card, pencils, crayons, scissors, felt-tipped pens, string, large paper-clips or pegs.

Preparation
Tie the string from one part of the room to the other, like a washing line.

What to do
Ask the children to look at what they are wearing today. Tell them that they are going to draw, colour and cut out pictures of their clothes, to peg onto the washing line.

The activity involves each child in completing the following tasks:

* drawing a garment quite large, colouring it in and then cutting it out;
* telling you what the garment is called and what sound it begins with;
* drawing a large letter appropriate to that sound on another piece of paper or card;
* pegging the letter to the line with its garment (with help from an adult).

Questions to ask
What are you wearing today? What is this called? Who has a sweatshirt on? Who is wearing leggings? Who is wearing jogging trousers? What else could we draw to put on the washing line? What do you have on your washing line at home? What sound does it begin with? What letter do you think that is? Can you draw or write the letter?

For younger children
Try to identify each child's level or stage of development. Some of them will need lots of help to get the shape of their letters right; some might need to trace or copy the letters.

For older children
Instead of putting the letters up with each individual item on the washing line, retain the letters and ask the children to identify the items on the line, then fit the letters to them.

Follow-up activities

* Help each small group of children to make an ABC frieze or booklet.
* If the children know all the individual letter sounds, move on to double consonants –'ch', 'sh' and 'st', for example.
* Sequence the tasks the other way round, so that each child draws a letter, says its sound, then draws, colours and cuts out something beginning with that letter that they might hang on the washing line.
* Together learn the song 'ABC Boogie' on photocopiable page 87.

Links with home

Send small alphabet friezes or alphabet books home with the children and ask parents or other adults to go carefully through the letters and the sounds they make, with them.

Tracing patterns

Learning outcome

To develop hand-eye co-ordination skills and develop left to right eye movement.

Group size
Four or five children.

What you need
Floor space in which to work, large pieces of paper (wallpaper would be appropriate), felt-tipped pens, pencils, crayons, a yellow highlighter pen.

Preparation
Lay the sheets of paper on the floor – you will need at least one for each child. Take one of the sheets of paper and make a pattern on it using straight lines, zigzag lines, curly patterns and so on. Draw the patterns in different colours and keep them ordered so that they can be 'read' from left to right and from top to bottom.

What to do
Explain to the children that you are going to draw patterns for them to trace individually. Let them look at the sheet of different patterns you have prepared, so that they can choose which patterns they would like you to do.

Draw about three different patterns on each sheet of paper to begin with – it is important to do this step of the activity with the children watching, as it gives you the opportunity to reinforce the idea of which corner of the paper they will start their writing, in which direction their writing implement will move, where they will go when they get to the end of the first line, and so on. Verbalise it as you are doing it, such as 'We're going to start in this corner and then go along this way...'

Before the children attempt any writing themselves, ask them to trace the patterns in the air; let them try to do the patterns as large as they can, by using their whole bodies; see if they can do them as tiny as they can, as though they were going to trace them on their hand.

Then allow the children lots of room to spread themselves out to trace over the patterns you have drawn on the paper. They should use big, sweeping movements when they are writing and physically move themselves from left to right to enable them to understand that the patterns are drawn in this direction.

Questions to ask
Where do we start? Which direction do we go in? What happens when we get to the edge of the paper? How do you hold your pencil/crayon/felt-tipped pen? Who can do their pattern in the air as big as a house? Who can do it as tiny as a mouse?

For younger children
To avoid confusing the children, it may be necessary to draw just one line of pattern for them.

For older children
Draw the lines of pattern in dots and ask them to join them up. They may be able to do a line of the pattern underneath yours by themselves.

Follow-up activities
* Trace over patterns which you have incorporated into paintings.
* Play 'Which pattern?': one child traces a pattern or a letter on another child's back, who then tries to guess what it is.
* Make a group pattern book with the children's work.
* Complete the photocopiable activity on page 94 – 'Follow the path'.
* Ask the children to draw the wheels to complete the pictures on photocopiable page 95, 'On the road'.

Links with home

Encourage parents to help the children to do writing patterns at home.

I sent a letter to my love

Learning outcome

To develop an awareness of some of the different purposes of writing.

Group size
Two or three children at a time, then whole group.

What you need
Space, paper, writing implements.

Preparation
Ensure that the children are well acquainted with your writing area, and know that there are many different things that can be written – letters, forms, stories, cards and so on.

What to do
Ask the children to decide on something that they would like to 'write'. It may be a letter, a story, an item for the diary, a shopping list – each child will have their own preference.

Let them choose appropriate paper and a writing implement and 'write' their piece of writing at their own stage of development. It may be that a child will draw a little picture and tell you what it's about, or make some marks on the paper and 'read' them to you. Help the children to fold their writing in half and write their name on the outside.

Collect the children's writing together, then sit in a circle to play 'I sent a letter to my love and on the way I dropped it'. Give one of the pieces of writing to a child and ask that child to take the 'letter' round the outside of the circle while the rest sing the song:

'I sent a letter to my love, and on the way I dropped it.' *(The child drops the letter behind someone.)*

'Someone must have picked it up and put it in their pocket.' *(The child nearest to the letter picks it up.)*

When the letter is dropped, tell the child who has picked up the letter to give it to you, so that you can help to read the name on the outside.

The child who has written the letter should then come out and say, 'My letter is a story/postcard/letter/list (whatever is appropriate)' and 'read' it to the group. He or she then has the next turn to drop a letter.

Questions to ask
What kind of writing do you want to do? Who are you writing it for? What kind of paper will you use? What will you choose to write with? Can you tell me what your writing says?

For younger children
The children may need to be reminded about what they have written; if necessary, make a short list when the children are doing their pieces of writing so that you can refer to it.

For older children
Some children will have made a good effort at writing the words they want to say but may find it difficult to read them back. Give them as much assistance and encouragement as you can.

Follow-up activities
* Display the pieces of writing with each child's name and, if possible, an accompanying brief explanation.
* Give the children access to as much writing as possible, so that they can explore its features and have something to imitate. For instance, take a photograph of them playing 'I sent a letter...', display it with the children's 'letters' and write a caption: 'We are all playing I sent a letter to my love. Can you see yourself?' Read it to the children and encourage them to respond.

Links with home

Encourage parents and other adults to do follow-up 'writing' with the children at home.

Letter snap

Learning outcome

To become familiar with the shapes and sounds of different letters.

Group size

Three or four children.

What you need

Card, black marker pen, pencils, crayons, felt-tipped pens, scissors.

Preparation

Cut the card into small pieces about the size of playing cards. You will need about 60 pieces of card. Draw a simple picture of something on half the cards, for example a fish, a cat, a book, a ball, a frog, a snail. (If you don't like drawing, cut out pictures from old magazines and glue them onto the cards.) The items on the cards should begin with letters that the children will recognise most easily, such as 'e', 's', 'h' or 't'; some of the letters will be doubled up, but that doesn't matter. Write the initial letter of each item in lower case on the back of the picture cards. Leave the rest of the cards blank.

What to do

Deal out the blank cards to the children. Hold the picture cards in your hand. Place one card, face up, on the table.

Display one picture card at a time, letting the children take it in turns to identify the picture and decide which sound and letter it begins with. If they can trace the letter in the air with their hand or one of their fingers they can write it on the blank card. Turn over the picture card so that the children can decide whether the letters match. If they do, the child gets both cards and puts them in a pile.

Continue until all the cards are used up. The child who has the most cards wins.

Questions to ask

What does this picture show? What sound does it begin with? Who knows what the letter is called? Can you trace the letter in the air?

For younger children

Give the children some help when they are identifying the letters by pointing out the letters on an alphabet frieze. The idea is not to try and 'trick' them but to help them to become familiar with the letters.

If they need help to write their letters, mark them faintly on the card so that they can trace over them.

For older children

Let the children write the letter on the blank card straight away, rather than tracing it in the air first. They can then check by turning over the picture card to see if they were correct.

Follow-up activities

* Play 'Letter snap' in pairs – one child has the picture cards, one the letters; they turn them over simultaneously and shout 'Snap' if the letter is correct for the picture. They must always check with the letter on the back of the picture before they collect the cards.
* Cut out letters from headings in magazines and sort them into individual piles, one for all the 'a's, one for the 'b's and so on.
* Play 'How many things can you think of beginning with...?' Hold up one letter and brainstorm a list.

Links with home

Suggest that magnetic letters on the fridge door can be used at home to help the children learn their sounds.

What shall we write?

Learning outcome

To develop interest and ability in writing.

Group size
Four or five children.

What you need
Resources for a writing corner including paper in different sizes and colours, writing implements, erasers, rulers, notebooks, envelopes, postcards, greetings cards, forms, message pads, an old typewriter, old diaries and calendars, gummed paper, stamps.

Preparation
Prepare an interesting writing corner with a table and chairs, and as many of the above resources as possible. Make a postbox for the children to post their pieces of writing. Put up a memo board to which notes can be pinned.

What to do
Most of the children will not be at a stage for formal writing lessons yet. The best thing you can do to encourage the children to enjoy writing and thus develop their writing skills is to be a good role model yourself. Therefore your first task is to talk enthusiastically about writing, 'Oh I'd like to send a postcard to so and so.' In this way the children will see that writing is not a chore but a pleasure and something that has its own function in real life.

Make sure that every child has a turn in the writing corner at least once or twice in each week and encourage them to sit with you and use the materials for their own enjoyment. They may want to write letters to friends, notes or memos, greetings cards, labels, jokes to each other, things to remember on the calendar or stories.

Whatever they want to write, encourage them and be positive about their abilities. Remember that young children are not born being able to write, it is a skill that they have to develop so don't be too concerned with spelling or neatness at this stage. Encourage their attempted spellings and give them lots of praise.

At this early age it is important that the children should learn how to hold their writing implements correctly, and that they should learn how to form letters in the correct way right from the beginning.

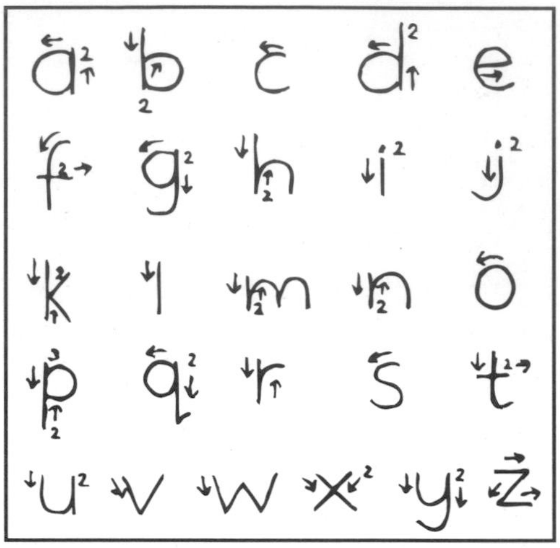

Questions to ask
What shall we write today? Who shall we write to? What shall we write about? Tell me what you're going to say. Show me where you're going to start. Read your writing to me.

For younger children
Give them lots of time to experiment with their writing. Help them to feel that their efforts are always valuable. Respond positively and sensitively to their endeavours.

For older children
The same comments apply whatever the age of the child but the older the children become the more they begin to realise that writing needs to be 'right' and they can easily become disillusioned with their own efforts. Avoid this happening at all costs.

Follow-up activities
* Help the children to make their own books.
* Post letters to the children, delivered by the postman.
* Encourage the children to share their writing with others in the group.

Links with home

Let children write their own invitations for parents and other adults to come into the group for open evenings or other events.

Alphabet pockets

Learning outcome

To learn the shapes of the letters of the alphabet.

Group size
Whole group.

What you need
Wallpaper or frieze paper, card, 26 envelopes (A4 size), scissors, collage materials such as gummed shapes, PVA adhesive/drawing-pins, glitter, screwed-up tissue paper, small pieces of fabric and so on.

Preparation
Pin the wallpaper or frieze paper up on the wall in a piece long enough for the envelopes to be fixed to it. Draw large hollow letter shapes onto card and cut them out. Do two or three letters for each child (if you have to go over the alphabet two or three times, that's fine). Label each envelope with a letter of the alphabet and pin or stick it to the wallpaper.

What to do
Give each child one letter shape, cut out of card, to start with. Help them to identify their letter and tell them to look closely at its shape – draw their attention to any spaces in the letter within its shape.

Help the children to use the collage materials to decorate their letter shapes, gluing them in place. Don't worry if bits go over the edge, they are still learning to get used to the shapes. Write the child's name on the back of each finished letter, so that the letters can be identified.

When all the letters are finished (this may take several sessions) collect the children together in a group. Call for the letters, naming them one by one, and encourage each child to come forward, show their letter and be praised for it. The letter then goes into the appropriate envelope.

If the children enjoy the activities you can do it with both upper and lower case letters but don't do them at the same time! Encourage the children to do the capital letters that begin their own names first to help them get used to them.

Questions to ask
See the shape of this letter – has it got curly bits? Has it got straight bits? Make its sound. How would you like to decorate it? How many 'a's have we got in the 'a' pocket?

For younger children
Help the children to trace the letter shapes with their fingers, making sure that they work in the direction in which the letter should be written.

For older children
Invite them to make the shape of the letters in the air – as large as they can as though they are painting with a huge brush and very small as though they are writing with a pinhead.

Follow-up activities
* Make collage pictures of the children's names.
* Play a sorting and matching game. Mix the letters up and let the children sort them into their appropriate envelopes.
* Make large templates of letters and suggest that the children draw round them and colour them in.

Links with home

Ask the children's parents and other adults to help them practise writing the letters of their names at home.

Tell me a story

Learning outcome

To develop the ability to sequence, remember and add to a story.

Group size
Whole group.

What you need
A flip chart or easel, a black marker pen.

What to do
Tell the children that you are going to do some 'shared writing' and ask them to sit on the carpet where they can all see the flip chart. Discuss what you might write – perhaps a story, a poem or a letter. Talk about who the writing will be for and what will happen to it when it's finished. Discuss how the writing might be presented.

Discuss the topic for writing. As a new venture, it might be as well to begin with a familiar story or write an account of something all the children have done together, such as a recent trip. This will mean that the writing you compose as a group will have a clear structure and all the children will be able to understand the sequencing.

The first step is to brainstorm all the ideas that are to be included in the writing. As the children give you suggestions, write them as a list on the flip chart.

When all the ideas have been offered, go through them and ask the children to help you to organise them into the order in which they should be written. Numbering each idea will give you a plan.

Begin the writing with whatever the children have decided should come first. Write a draft of the first sentence, read it to the children, showing them that print is read from left to right. If they want to change the sentence, cross it out and redraft it. Continue until you reach a natural end for the writing.

Questions to ask
What word do we need to begin this sentence? What happens next? What could we put in here? Who remembers what this first sentence said? What should happen next? Which bit is that on the list?

For younger children
Copy out the text onto sugar paper in whatever format is appropriate and let the children illustrate it. It is important that the children feel 'ownership' of this writing even though you have been the scribe. They will learn that the composition and the writing are both important parts of the writing process.

For older children
The completed text can be copied out by the children to make individual books or letters. The shared writing experience will help them to understand about the permanence of text and how it helps people to remember ideas.

Follow-up activities
* Make the shared writing experience a regular one; the children will get better at composing with practice and will understand the connection between composition and script.
* When writing stories, add small sections to them in further sessions, so that you are continually recapping and re-reading what has gone before and adding to the sequence of events.
* Let the children compose stories, letters and other forms of writing in small groups, returning to you to help them to do the scribing.

Links with home

Send the stories, poems, letters and so on home for the children to share with their families.

Photocopiable assessment sheet

Speaking and Listening

Name ______________________________

	Assessment and comments					
Skills and concepts	**Baseline/1st assessment**	**Date**	**2nd assessment**	**Date**	**End of year assessment**	**Date**
Sits quietly and listens to story						
Follows a simple instruction						
Can follow two (or more) instructions						
Listens attentively and responds to rhymes/songs						
Volunteers responses to discussion						
Initiates conversation with peers						
Initiates conversation with adults						
Joins in group discussion appropriately						

Photocopiable assessment sheet

Reading

Name ______________________

	Assessment and comments					
Skills and concepts	Baseline/1st assessment	Date	2nd assessment	Date	End of year assessment	Date
Holds book appropriately						
Turns pages appropriately						
Tells story from memory						
Uses memory to match familiar words						
Recognises some letters by shape or sound						
Can read familiar words in a range of contexts, such as own name						
Can read simple texts, labels, signs and so on						

Writing

Name ______________________________

Skills and concepts	Assessment and comments					
	Baseline/1st assessment	**Date**	**2nd assessment**	**Date**	**End of year assessment**	**Date**
Understands that print has meaning						
Uses symbols and identifiable letters in communication						
Writes own name with appropriate letters						
Hears sounds in words and writes corresponding letters in sequence						
Attempts to write in sentences						
Attempts to spell new words						

Letter home

Dear parents and carers

Please show your children that reading is an important and enjoyable thing to do. When you read to them, they learn a lot more than what is happening in the story. They absorb how to hold and handle a book, how to turn the pages and how a story can be told. Their curiosity in the words and pictures is the first step towards reading. They enjoy guessing what will happen next, and what the pictures will show. They find it fun to anticipate the words and to join in with sections that are repeated.

This is how to read to your children:

* Make sure you have a quiet time and place, with no distractions.
* Be comfortable; promote a feeling of closeness.
* Read every day. Ten minutes a day is better than an hour once a month and they will look forward to your shared reading times.
* Read slowly in a relaxed voice, using as much expression as you can.
* Draw their attention to words that are repeated frequently, and encourage them to join in.
* Ask questions – what do you think will happen next? Why do you think that happened? Give plenty of time for response.
* The public library is an excellent source of books and you'll find plenty of material appropriate to your children's interests.
* Read lots of different kinds of books – wordless books, lift-the-flap books, pop-up books, nursery rhyme books, alphabet books.
* Help your children to explore picture story books and to recognise and label objects from their own experiences.
* Read their favourites to them over and over again.

Sharing books with your children every day can become a very happy habit. It will enable them to develop language experience, and it will set them on course for learning to read. You'll probably enjoy it yourself, too!

Yours sincerely

Kitchen sink sounds

Tap goes *drip drip*
plip plip plink.
Tap goes *trickle*
at the kitchen sink.

Plates go *clatter.*
Pans go *slop.*
Spoons go *clink clink.*
Bubbles go *POP!*

Tony Mitton

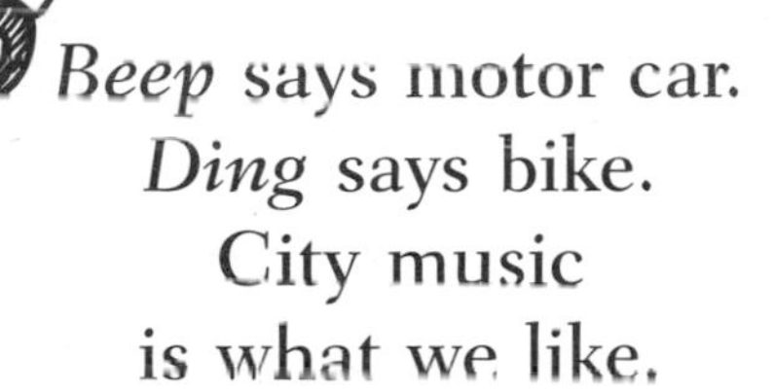

Listen around

Beep says motor car.
Ding says bike.
City music
is what we like.

Buzz says busy bee.
Bird says *Tweet.*
Garden music
is soft and sweet.

Moo says cow.
Neigh says horse.
Farmyard music
is best, of course.

What's **your** best,
your favourite sound?
Open your ears
and listen around.

Tony Mitton

Finger face

This little finger's got a smile upon its face,
this second finger looks as though it's in disgrace,
finger number three has got a very cheeky grin
but the fourth looks as though it's sitting on a drawing-pin
and the fifth one along is looking lonely, looking glum
because it's not a finger like the others. It's a thumb!

Gina Douthwaite

Begins with 'B'

A bear?
A box?
A bin?
A bush?

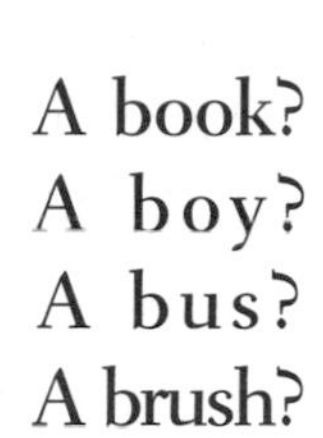

A book?
A boy?
A bus?
A brush?

A basket?
Boot? A bit
of bread? A
bone? A bench?
A bouncy bed?

A badger's boil?
A blackbird's beak?
A bun? A bottom?
Building brick?

A bad banana?
Broken brolly? Biscuit
bitten by a bully?

Bubbles bursting in a
beaker? Bonny baby?
Bloomers? Beaver?

Bunch of bluebells?
Bee? A blot?
What is this shape?
What have I got?

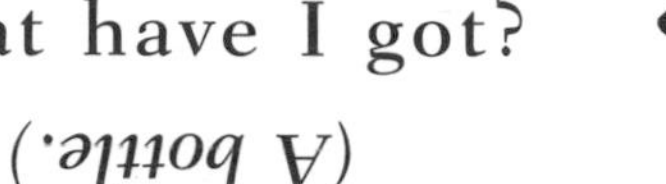

(A bottle.)

Gina Douthwaite

Mouse

Mouse
in a hedge
scurries
up a twig,
leaps like
a lion
brave and big,
clings to a leaf
that's spinning
round and round,
mouse in a hedge is
dizzy off the ground,
drops into daffodils,
ripples through the
grass, scurries up a
twig again.
S p
r
i
n
g
a
t
l
a
s
t.

Gina Douthwaite

The house that Jack built

This is the house that Jack built.

This is the malt
that lay in the house that Jack built.

This is the rat
that ate the malt
that lay in the house that Jack built.

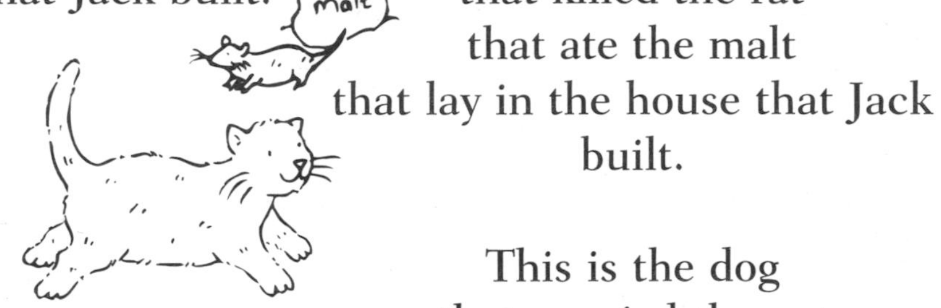

This is the cat
that killed the rat
that ate the malt
that lay in the house that Jack
built.

This is the dog
that worried the cat
that killed the rat
that ate the malt
that lay in the house that Jack
built.

This is the cow with the crumpled horn
that tossed the dog
that worried the cat
that killed the rat
that ate the malt
that lay in the house that Jack built.

This is the maiden all forlorn
that milked the cow with the crumpled
horn
that tossed the dog
that worried the cat
that killed the rat
that ate the malt
that lay in the house that Jack built.

This is the man all tattered and torn
that kissed the maiden all forlorn
that milked the cow with the
crumpled horn
that tossed the dog
that worried the cat
that killed the rat
that ate the malt
that lay in the house that Jack built.

This is the priest all shaven and shorn
that married the man all tattered and torn
that kissed the maiden all forlorn
that milked the cow with the crumpled horn
that tossed the dog
that worried the cat
that killed the rat
that ate the malt
that lay in the house that Jack built.

This is the cock
that crowed in the morn
that waked the priest all shaven and shorn
that married the man all tattered and torn
that kissed the maiden all forlorn
that milked the cow with the crumpled horn
that tossed the dog
that worried the cat
that killed the rat
that ate the malt
that lay in the house that Jack built.

This is the farmer sowing his corn
that kept the cock
that crowed in the morn
that waked the priest all shaven and shorn
that married the man all tattered and torn
that kissed the maiden all forlorn
that milked the cow with the crumpled horn
that tossed the dog
that worried the cat
that killed the rat
that ate the malt
that lay in the house that Jack built.

Trad. Retold by Irene Yates

The engine driver

The train goes running along the line,
Jicketty-can, jicketty-can.
I wish it were mine, I wish it were mine,
Jicketty-can, jicketty-can.
The engine driver stands in front –
He makes it run, he makes it shunt;

Out of the town,
Out of the town,
Over the hill,
Over the down,
Under the bridges,
Across the lea,
Over the ridges
And down to the sea,

With a jicketty-can, jicketty-can,
Jicketty-jicketty-jicketty-can,
Jicketty-can, jicketty-can...

Clive Sansom

Hissssss

Say –
sticklebacks,
spiders,
snowflakes in space,
Say –
squiggles
and spatters
and spots-on-your-face,
Say –
scarecrows
and scattergrows,
snuggles and sea –
S is the letter that says
sssssssssss to me!

Irene Yates

Silent Simon

Everyone was getting worried about Simon because he wouldn't talk. If anyone asked him a question he answered by nodding or shaking his head and if he wanted anything he pointed to it.

'It's time Simon talked,' said Aunt Kate. 'He's almost four now.'

Mum sighed and looked at Simon playing with his train set. 'I know. And I'm sure he *can* talk. But he won't. I don't know why.'

Simon carried on playing with his trains and pretended he hadn't heard. But he felt sad. He wanted to talk. He really did. Words were always bustling around in his head, the trouble was, he didn't know how to say them. That's why he didn't talk. He didn't want to sound silly.

'Oh well, never mind,' said Aunt Kate. She looked over at Simon. 'Do you want to come swimming, Simon?' she asked.

Simon nodded eagerly. He got his swimming things, waved goodbye to Mum and set off with Aunt Kate.

The water was lovely and warm. Simon splashed around happily. Aunt Kate threw a big ball to him. 'Catch!' she said, but the ball floated away. Some children started to play with it. Simon watched the children laughing as they threw the ball to each other. 'It's my ball,' he thought. 'My ball.' The words were going round and round in his head, then suddenly they popped out. 'My ball!' he shouted. 'It's my ball.'

'Oh, sorry,' said a little girl. She threw the ball over to him. 'Here you are.'

'Thank you,' said Simon, glad to have his ball back.

Then he noticed some children going down a slide into the water. It looked fun. He looked at Aunt Kate and pointed to the slide. She didn't say anything, so he climbed out of the pool and started to walk over to the slide.

'Where are you going, Simon?' called Aunt Kate.

Simon pointed over at the slide and carried on walking.

But Aunt Kate shouted again. 'Where are you going, Simon?'

Suddenly the words popped out. 'The slide,' Simon told her.

Aunt Kate smiled. 'Go on then, I'll catch you at the bottom,' she told him.

Simon climbed up the steps to the slide and slid right down into the water with a big SPLASH!

'Got you!' laughed Aunt Kate.

'Again!' shouted Simon.

Simon wanted to stay in the swimming pool all day, but soon it was time to go home. 'Your mum will be wondering where we are,' Aunt Kate said.

'Just one more slide?' begged Simon. 'Please!'

After three more slides they went home.

Mum was in the garden. 'Did you have a nice time?' she asked.

'Smashing!' said Simon. 'But I'm thirsty. Can I have a drink?'

Mum stared at him in surprise. 'Er... yes. There's some pop in the fridge,' she said.

'Thanks,' said Simon, running inside.

'How did you get him to speak?' Mum asked Aunt Kate.

Aunt Kate's eyes twinkled. 'I think he realised that he had more fun if he spoke,' she said.

In the kitchen, Simon poured himself a drink of pop and smiled happily. Talking hadn't been so bad after all! He'd have to do it more often.

Karen King

Pots and tripes

Susie S decided she would have a day off. 'I'm fed up doing esses here and esses there all day long.'

She curled up into a little cosy s-shape in her bed.

But the rest of the folk in ABC Village didn't sleep. Oh no.

Mister M was decorating. Slosh, slosh, slosh he went with his paintbrush. But instead of sloshing it only loshed.

'I'll put up my wallpaper instead!' Mister M muttered.

The wallpaper was yellow. With red and green spots and stripes. At least, it was like that when he bought it yesterday. Now it was yellow, with red and green pots and tripes.

In the village shop, little Billy B was buying his lunch. Salami and salad sandwiches, with satsumas for sweet.

But all the shopkeeper, Walter W, could winkle out of his wooden boxes was alami and alad andwiches and atumas for weet.

'Whoever heard of such a thing!' cried Billy B.

Just then, into the shop marched Mister M. 'You told me this wallpaper was yellow with red and green spots and stripes and look at it!' He rolled out the paper. There it was. Pots and tripes.

'Say seaside,' Billy B said.

'Ea-ide!' said Walter W and Mister M both together.

'Susie S must have gone back to bed!' said Billy.

Susie S was surprised when they knocked at her door. But she didn't mind. 'I couldn't sleep properly anyway,' she said, 'I could only leep.'

Then they all sat down to a nice cup of tea and strawberry shortcakes. 'Actually,' Mister M said, after his sixth strawberry shortcake, 'I was quite getting to like those pots and tripes.' And everybody laughed.

Irene Yates

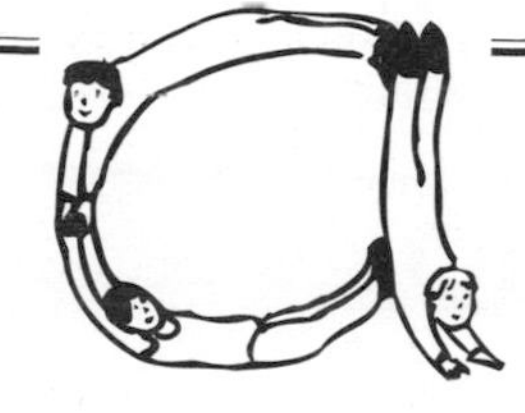

The alphabet hunt

'We've been learning the alphabet at nursery today,' Natasha told her dad.

'That's good,' he said. 'Tell me it then.'

'A, b, c... er...' Natasha frowned. 'I've forgotten it,' she said.

'Abcdefghijklmnopqrstuvwxyz,' Dad said.

Natasha tried it. 'A, B, C, D, E, G, S...' She shook her head. 'Too many letters,' she sighed. 'I'll never remember them all.'

'Course you will,' said Dad. 'Come on, we'll go on an alphabet hunt. We have to find something beginning with each letter of the alphabet.'

He wrote the alphabet on a piece of paper and gave it to Natasha. 'First we'll look for something beginning with A,' he said. 'Can you see anything?'

Natasha looked around the room. 'No,' she said.

'What about in the fruit bowl?' asked Dad.

Natasha looked at the fruit. 'A is for apple!' she shouted.

'That's right,' said Dad, helping her to tick the letter A. 'Now let's look for something beginning with B.'

'Easy!' grinned Natasha. 'B for bowl!'

'Well done,' said Dad. They ticked B. 'Now C. C is for...'

'Cat!' shouted Natasha as Smudge, their cat, strolled past. 'And D is for door!'

Dad smiled. 'I bet you can't see anything beginning with E.'

'Yes I can. E is for egg!' said Natasha. 'And F for fruit!'

Dad said, 'And G is for?'

'Girl!' Natasha pointed to herself. She looked at the list to see what the next letter was. 'H is for hair!' She frowned. 'But I can't see anything beginning with I.'

'Let's go into the garden, we might find something there,' suggested Dad.

So they went into the garden. 'I is for insect!' Natasha said, pointing to a tiny insect scurrying across the ground.

'What about J?' asked Dad. He jumped up and down, and the keys on his belt jangled.

Natasha laughed. 'J for jump!' she said. 'And K for keys!'

Natasha looked at the alphabet again. 'L is for leg, M for mouth and N for nose!' She pointed to each of them in turn. 'Now it's your go, Dad. Find something beginning with O.'

Dad grinned. 'O is for... onion!' He picked an onion out of the vegetable patch.

'And P is for pea!' said Natasha. 'But what about Q?'

Dad picked some daisies, made them into a crown and put it on Natasha's head. 'Q is for queen!' he told her.

Natasha giggled and looked at the list again. 'R is for rose, S is for sun and T is for tree!' she said. 'Now you do U and V!'

'Mmm, well U is for us.' Dad pointed to him and Natasha. 'And V is for vase!' he added, pointing to the vase of flowers in the window.

'And W is for window!' Natasha said. 'But what about X?' They both looked and looked but they couldn't find anything beginning with X.

Just then, Mum came out to join them.

'We can't find anything beginning with an X,' Natasha said.

'I can!' smiled Mum, and fetched Natasha's xylophone from her bedroom. 'X is for xylophone,' said Mum.

'And Y is for you!' said Dad, pointing to Mum.

'And Z is for zip!' said Natasha, showing them the zip on her top.

'Well, that's the alphabet hunt finished, so let's say the alphabet one more time,' said Dad. 'All together now ... abcdefghijklmnopqrstuvwxyz!'

And this time Natasha said it all the way through.

Karen King

Tell me a story, little book

Johanne Levy

ABC Boogie

Verse 2

a for apple, b for ball,
Curly c comes next.
d e f g
h for hat
i j and here comes the rest.

4.
A
-bet

Verse 3

Kicking k and l for leg.
m n o p q
r for run
And s for sun
t u v w x y z.

Verse 4

a for ant
And e for egg
i for Internet
o for orange
u for up
Make the vowels of the alphabet.

Johanne Levy

What can we do?

Say what each child is doing.

Who are we? (P33)

Hey diddle diddle

Cut out these pictures and stick them in the right order.

Can you say the nursery rhyme?

Reading pictures (P45)

Animal sounds

What sounds do these animals make?

Animal sounds (P46)

Boots match

Colour and match the boots.

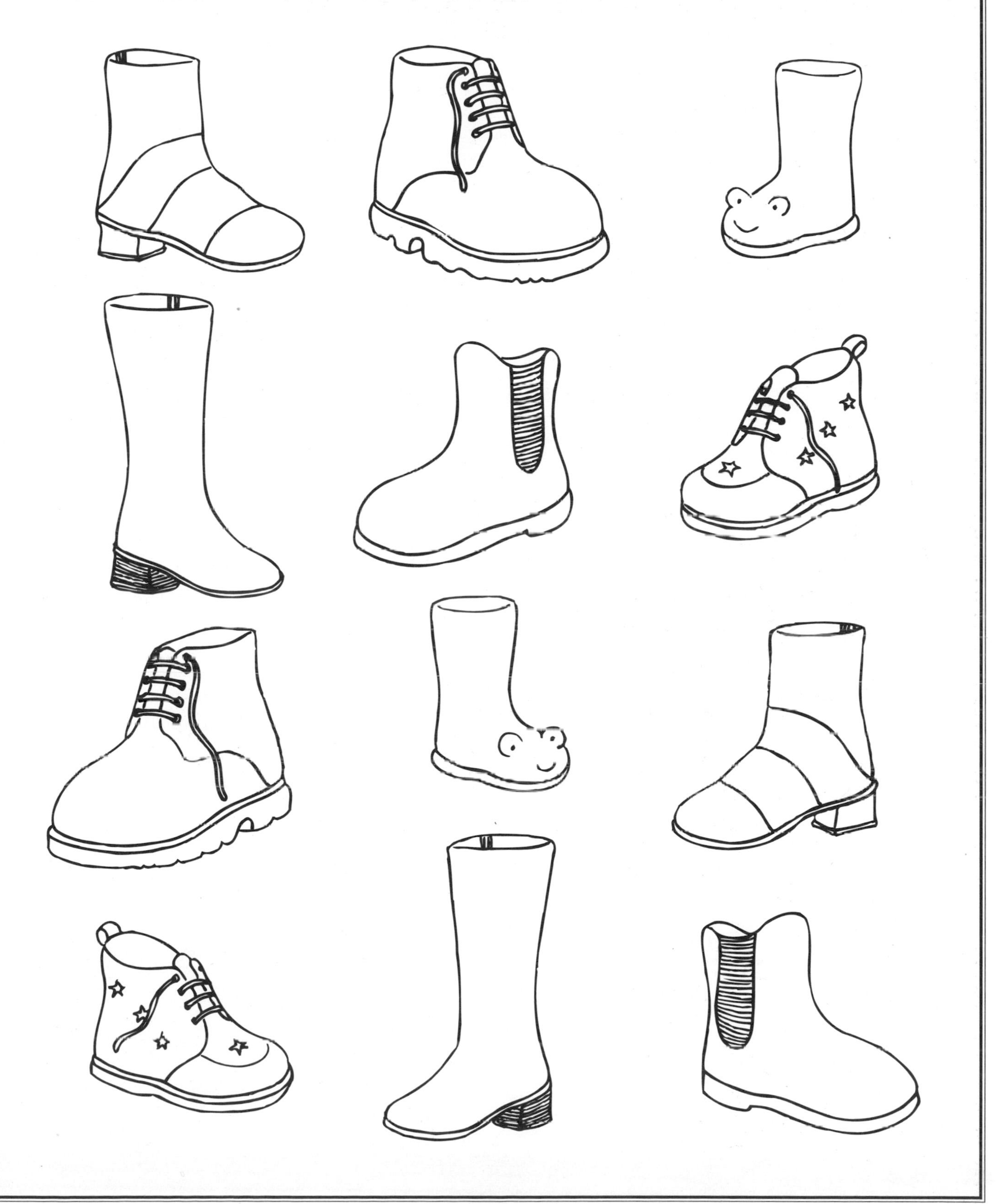

Let's match (P48)

Look for 's'

Name these things.

Colour the things that begin with the sound of 's'.

I can... (P52), Pictures and sounds (P63)

Make a story

Make a story for each row by saying words where you see the arrows.

Colour the pictures.

Help with the story (P61)

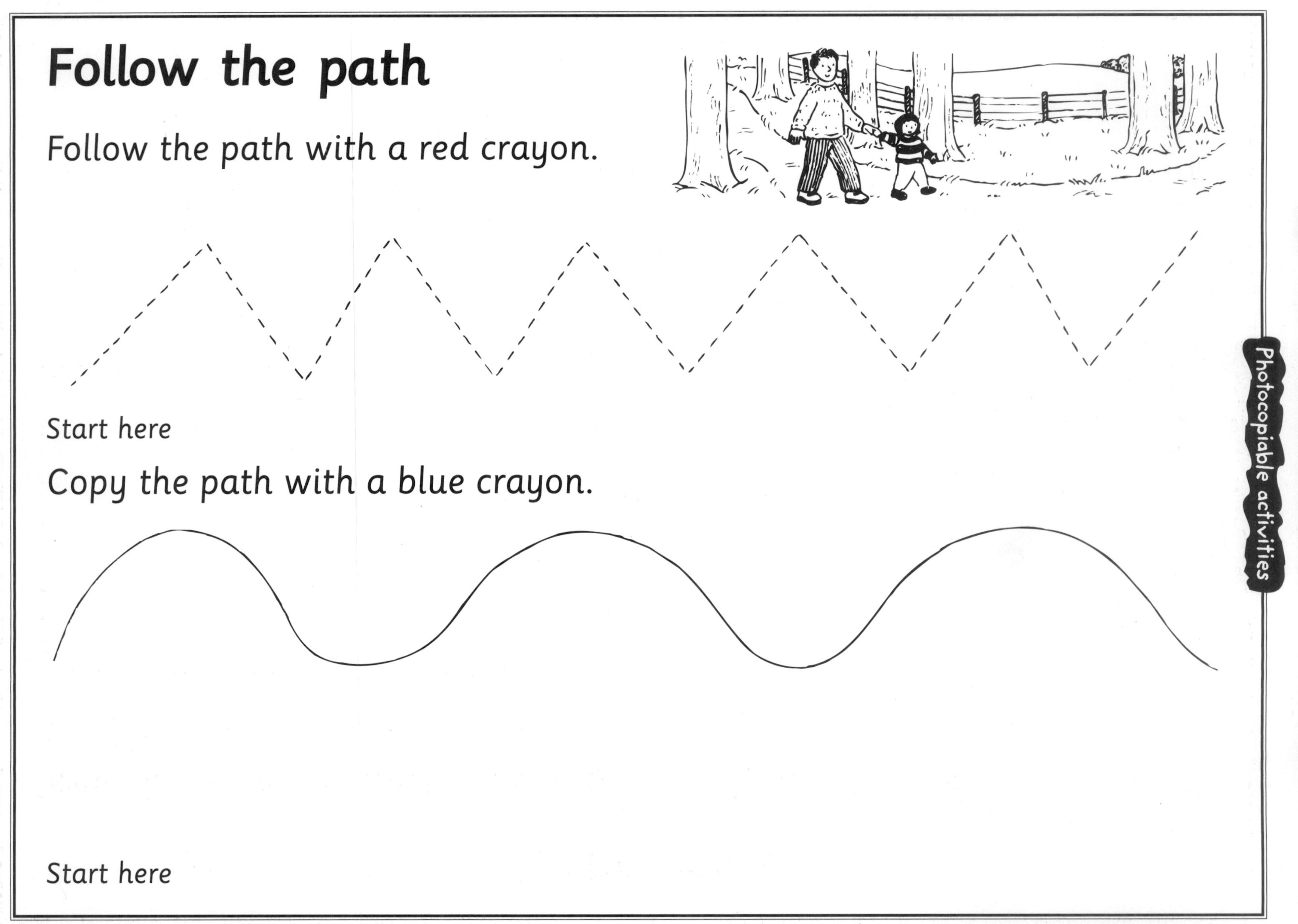

Tracing patterns (P67)

On the road

Draw the wheels on the lorry and car. Put them on a road.

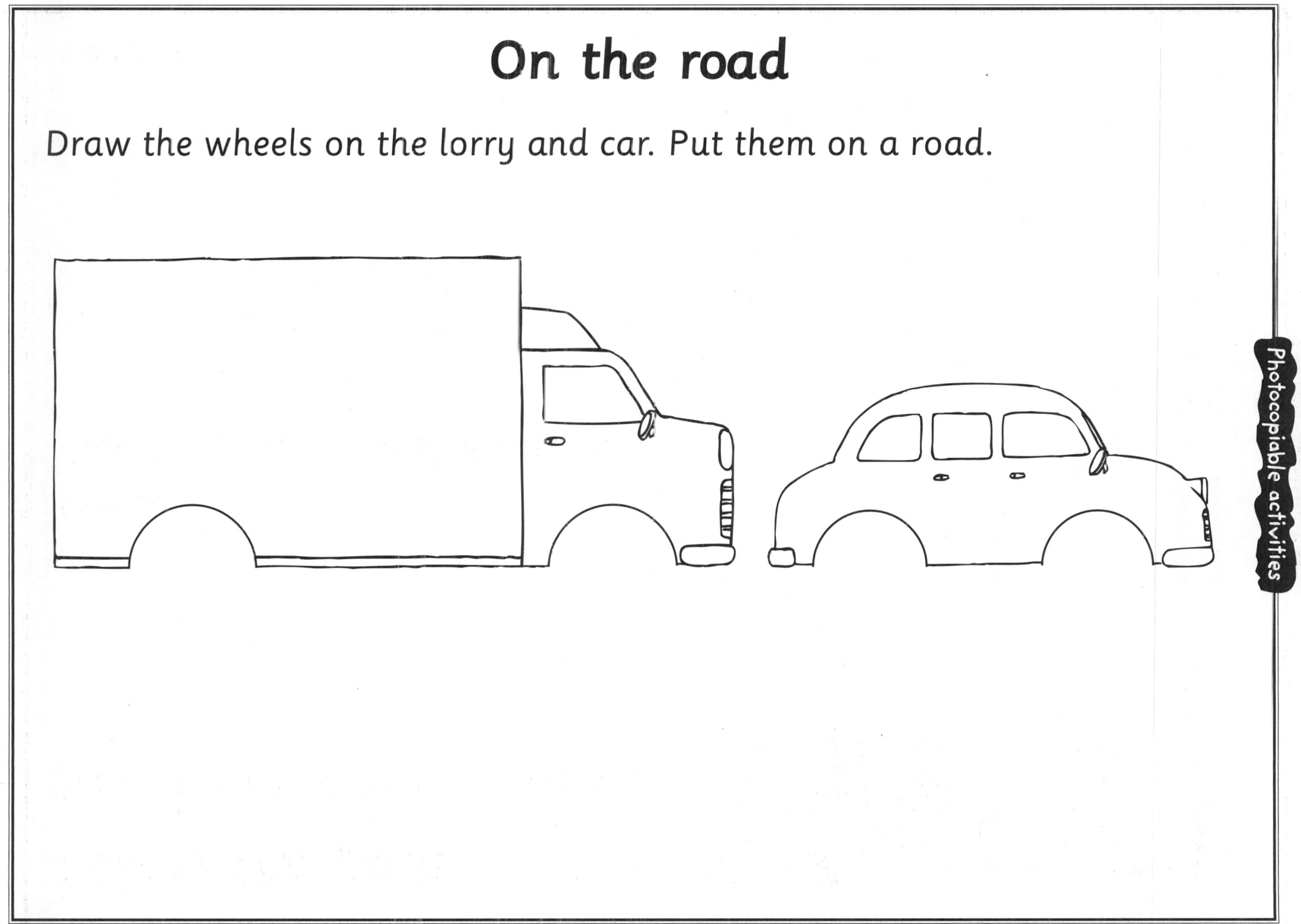

Tracing patterns (P67)

Further reading

Listening to Children Reading Helen Arnold (Hodder & Stoughton).

Learning Together Through Talk: Key Stages 1 and 2 edited by Gordon Baddeley (Hodder & Stoughton).

Learning to Read with Picture Books Jill Bennett (The Thimble Press).

Babies Need Books Dorothy Butler (Penguin).

Writing: Teachers and Children at Work Donald Graves (Heinemann Educational).

Good Reading Guide to Children's Books Christina Koning (Bloomsbury).

Listen to your Child David Crystal (Penguin).

Language and Literacy in the Early Years Marian Whitehead (Paul Chapman Publishing).

Useful addresses

The Thimble Press
Lockwood, Station Road, South Woodchester, Stroud, Glos GL5 5EQ
Publishes the journal ***Signal*** and other writing about children's literature and literacy.

The School Library Association
Liden Library, Barrington Close, Liden, Swindon, Wiltshire SN3 6HF
Scotland: Education Centre, Castle Street, Dingwall IV15 9HU

Federation of Children's Book Groups
6 Bryce Place, Currie, Edinburgh EH14 5LR
Publishes booklists including ***Pick of the Year*** (50 top titles chosen for the Children's Book Award) and organises National Tell a Story Week.

British Association of Early Childhood Education (BAECE)
111 City View House, 463 Bethnal Green Road, London E2 9QY

Pre-school Learning Alliance (PLA)
69 Kings Cross Road, London WC1X 9LL

Letterbox Library
Unit 2D, Leroy House, 436 Essex Road, London N1 3QP
A mail order book club that specialises in non-sexist and multicultural books for children.

School Bookshop Association
6 Brightfield Road, Lee, London SE12 8QF
Publishes ***Books for Keeps*** magazine.

Soma Books
38 Kennington Lane, London SE11 4LS
Multicultural bookshop that sells dual texts.

Tamarind
PO Box 296, Camberley, Surrey GU15 4WD
Specialises in early years picture books including those that give a positive profile to black children.

Young Book Trust
Book House, 45 East Hill, London SW18 2QZ
Has a store of information about books for children and publishes booklists for under-fives.

Write to the following address for a catalogue of other early years teaching resources:

Scholastic Ltd
Marketing Department
Villiers House
Clarendon Avenue
Leamington Spa
Warwickshire CV32 5PR